ATHEISM

RELIGION

and

LIFE

(A Layman's Perspective)

by

Brian Hinkley

Lulu 2015

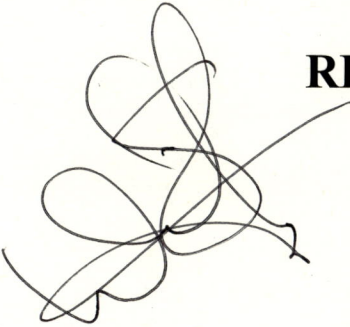

Atheism Religion and Life
(A Layman's Perspective)

Printed in the United States of America

Published by Lulu.com

ISBN: 978-1-312-97868-3

Dedication

This book is dedicated to the layman.

Layman:

"A person without professional or specialized knowledge in a particular subject."

www.facebook.com/atheismreligionandlife

Email: atheismreligionandlife@outlook.com

Acknowledgements

To all the everyday people I've met through life's journey who taught me humility. Their frank honesty and sincerity demonstrated a quality of humanity not always found in the upper echelons of society. I am forever grateful for those who can be forthright and candid, without hatred or animus.

For someone who has never written a book, the aid and assistance from others is invaluable. No words could adequately express my appreciation for those who assisted me in what initially seemed like a crazy idea.

Both believers and non-believers helped in reviewing the initial manuscript for this book, and the many redrafts and corrections, which seemed never-ending. It is always difficult to know where to start when acknowledging friends, family and professional colleagues. In no particular order, I want to specifically thank some very special people.

I had the pleasure of working with Susan Reeder while serving on Hamilton City Council. Susan was always loyal, dedicated and meticulous. Her many suggestions, as well as correcting my many errors in the first draft of this book, was greatly appreciated.

My motorcycle buddies James Wiltshire (aka Popeye) and Charlie Faucher do not candy-coat their comments. They are direct without any B.S. Beverley Wiltshire is just too nice and let me down easy, but provided the kind of input that is extremely valuable.

My son, Jason (Jay), has definite opinions on the hypocrisy of religion. I'm glad my boy is a freethinker, and not afraid to speak his mind. Thanks, Jay, for helping with this book.

Anne Stewart is a remarkable woman. She is intelligent, dedicated to her community, and has a principled outlook on life. She says she is spiritual. I say she is a true humanist. Her life experience and insights were invaluable, as she understood the essence of this book.

My stepson, Michael, with a background in marketing, made me rethink the book's cover design and message. Thanks Mike. Now, don't forget to read the entire book.

Bobby (aka Bobby C.) is a man after my heart. He, along with the unrepentant Ms. Ashley, both of *"No Religion Required"* podcast fame, know the common person and the challenges ordinary people face in life. These two are real and genuine. They are working people. Their input is the kind that only a layman truly appreciates.

Charlene Farnsworth is a charming woman with a radiant personality. I met Charlene recently through a local atheist group. I thought it was important to have someone review my work who did not have a long association with me. She loved the book and provided a special kind of insight

The one person who knows all my faults is my wife, Ollie. We spent hours reviewing, line by line, the book's manuscript. Ollie made more corrections than I will ever admit. It was exhausting and frustrating, but in the end we passed the test. We still continue with our marital bliss.

And finally, how can I appropriately thank Professor Christopher DiCarlo for writing the Foreword to this book? I am very much indebted to him for his kind words of support.

~

Foreword

Brian Hinkley's book offers a candid account by critically examining and explaining Biblical scripture as well as a consideration of some of the entailments which might follow if one were to actually accept such ideas as Gospel. And he does this not in the language of the academic or the intellectual, but in the vernacular of the everyday person. This allows for a very natural delivery in what often reads as an extended internal dialogue between Brian and the theist.

With a capacity to reach the layperson, Hinkley chooses highly relevant passages from Biblical text to illustrate the inconsistencies, contradictions, and often down-right nastiness of the content of various passages from Scripture. In this manner, Brian offers a healthy dose of careful reflection which may well induce considerable cognitive dissonance amongst some true believers.

Brian does not pull punches when it comes to overt criticism of many Biblical passages. This can allow Christian readers who might have questions about their own personal faith, to rethink the role religion plays in today's society. Hinkley devotes considerable time considering some of the most harmful consequences the Abrahamic faiths can have on the individual and the damage which can be inflicted on the cultural, political and economic life of the world's population.

Drawing on his personal experience, Hinkley considers some of the arguments for and against religious dogma, atheism, and life. His arguments are presented using a number of different styles and approaches – some of which are quite imaginative – but always geared towards the layman. His use of humour and irreverent commentary assists the reader to place questionable biblical events, and the confusing language of the Bible, in a fashion that helps the ordinary person understand religious belief from an atheist's point of view.

By carefully considering some of the more questionable claims made by various religions – predominantly Christianity – Hinkley simplifies the complicated language that does more to confuse and obscure the reader, than clarify. Towards this end, Brian critiques Biblical passages by selectively examining specific sections of the Bible that most of the public are completely unfamiliar.

This book is provocative and offers one man's personal insights which will intrigue both the religious and non-religious. It is presented as a book for the layman, in layman's language. It is concise, easy to read, and understandable.

Whether you agree or disagree with the contents of this book, it is an important contribution in keeping the dialogue going which itself, is an extension of a fair society which allows for freedom of speech and a healthy amount of philosophical disagreement.

Christopher DiCarlo

Dr. Christopher DiCarlo is a fellow, advisor, and board member of the **Society of Ontario Free Thinkers.** He has addressed numerous national and international conferences and written many scholarly papers ranging from bioethics to cognitive evolution. His book entitled *How to Become a Really Good Pain in the Ass: A Critical Thinker's Guide to Asking the Right Questions,* was released world-wide by Prometheus Books in July 2011.

Comments from Readers

"A memorable book to open one's mind. I don't have to agree, but it helps in my quest for answers."

"I was disgusted to discover how women and young girls were subjugated. (which still happens today in some culture/religions)."

"A lot of research, good writing and thought-provoking."

"I knew 'God' was a murderous scum bag but was never aware of the extent. Also I knew he revered men and degraded women but I didn't know it was to the point that he'd put greater value on a donkey than a female."

"It simplified the Bible passages for me."

"I really enjoyed reading the Arbitration Award, it put the whole issue in perspective."

"Your analysis of the 'Sermon on the Mount' is golden. I had no idea."

"A provocative read about one man's journey from Christianity to Atheism."

"I enjoyed reading your interpretation of the Bible. You made it plain and simple to understand."

"I remember in Sunday school about the 'Walls of Jericho come tumbling down;' but I was never told about the genocide committed by God's warriors – hideous."

"You have written so much that I agree with that I lifted the following passage from your book and had it framed in my computer."

It reads as follows:

"Things happen in this world for no good or bad reason. In the case of the natural world, if lightning were to strike a toddler riding his tricycle, it was neither the devil nor a god that sent the deadly bolt of lightning. Nature is indifferent. It is random. The world isn't intrinsically hostile, or intrinsically safe. It doesn't care, and it doesn't play favourites."

"Terrific read, but I wish you had written more about how religion has fleeced billions of dollars from some of the most vulnerable and gullible in our society."

I agree with the reader who made the above comment, but this book was not focused on the greed of religion. The following quote from one of histories greatest freethinkers may ease this reader's positive criticism.

"All national institutions of churches, whether Jewish, Christian, or Turkish, appear to me no other than human inventions set up to terrify and enslave mankind, and monopolize power and profit."

—Thomas Paine

~

CONTENTS

~

"Science flies you to the moon. Religion flies you into buildings."

—Victor Stenger,
American physicist, philosopher, author, and religious skeptic.

Warning and Disclaimer

Please be warned this book contains explicit content. Some people will find the Bible stories and excerpts from the Bible upsetting. There are sections of this book that contain passages from the Bible that most, whether they attend church or not, will not have heard. I am not responsible for the actions, commands or events that God, Jesus or the so-called prophets committed. I am just spreading the message contained in the "Good Book."

I do accept responsibility for my comments, understanding and interpretation of these Bible passages in the same way as others over the millennia have also attempted to interpret the Bible. I suspect that some believers will find my comments and interpretation to be offensive, crude and sacrilegious. If you are religious, and you happen to read this entire book, I expect at some point you will be offended. If you find that parts of this book struck a nerve and raised your emotions, then I have accomplished something that may cause you to think.

For those who have never read the Bible in spite of its wide circulation (who, by the way, are the overwhelming majority of the world's population), I encourage you to read the entire Bible. Yes, as an atheist, I encourage you to read the entire Bible, not just selected passages. While you are reading the Bible, try to understand and comprehend what is being said. Try to visualize the actual events and happenings as they are described in the Bible. If you read the Bible dispassionately, and this means analytically, without emotion and being completely neutral, you cannot help but wonder how any thinking human being could believe any of this is true.

Statistics will vary, but most information suggests the majority of Canadians are Christians, with the Catholic Church having the most adherents. Christians represent approximately 67 percent of the population, and are followed by people with no religion at 24 percent. Islam is the second-largest religion in Canada, practised by 3.2 percent of the population. The balance is represented by various other religions.

While the statistics above may be close to the official statistics, I cannot prove my assumption that the real figures are more like the following:

- 15 percent diehard Christians
- 30 percent Sunday Christians (they don't practise Christianity)
- 20 percent lying Christians (don't practise or believe, but claim to be Christian)
- 30 percent non-believers of various stripes
- 5 percent various religious sects

Americans, I believe, would have a much larger percentage of believers. However, recent studies have shown that the single-largest growing sector, in both Canada and the United States, is the non-believers. If the readers of this book were equally divided on a prorated basis, here is my prediction.

Making the most optimistic assumption — with the provision that those who read this book and put some effort into reading the Bible and dispassionately reading the books I have recommended, along with checking out the recommended websites and podcasts — a seismic shift would take place in the thinking of people.

The results would shift the previously quoted statistics along these lines:

- 14 percent diehard Christians
- 20 percent Sunday Christians (they don't practise Christianity)
- 10 percent lying Christians (don't practise or believe, but claim to be Christian)
- 52 percent non-believers of various stripes
- 4 percent various religious sects

Knowledge is a wonderful and powerful thing. The acquisition of knowledge makes people think. People who think start to ask questions. Inquiring minds challenge what they are told. The church and religion are built on a foundation of accepted beliefs. Religion, for a long time, had a privileged position in our society. It held a status that placed it above critical scrutiny. Any overt disagreement with religious doctrine was viewed as an attack. They called it sacrilegious or blasphemous. Even today, in some religions, the penalty for such utterances is death.

Since the 9-11 attack and the birth of the *"New Atheism,"* these religious myths and beliefs are being questioned as never before. For the religious readers of this book, I therefore issue this warning. The reading of this book may make you think. It may make you question your faith in the supernatural. It may cause you, initially, some anxiety. Just remember, you, and you alone, are responsible for your reactions. I disclaim any responsibility if it causes you emotional pain. Growth can sometimes be painful. On the other hand, growth can be liberating.

I have found that shedding my religious beliefs were just that...liberating. It liberated me of guilt, fear, shame and hypocrisy. Once I got this monkey off my back, I felt freedom and relief. Not the kind of freedom that makes one wild. But the kind of freedom that removes chains that bind.

I have discovered total freedom of thought and a new humanism toward mankind. I know there is both good and evil in this world. I want to do good. Religion, I find, has done both good and evil to society, but on balance, it has done far more evil than good. I do not need a god to be a good person; neither do you.

"With or without religion, you would have good people doing good things and evil people doing evil things. But for good people to do evil things, that takes religion."

—Steven Weinberg

~

Introduction

"Reason and science aligns itself with common sense; religion and superstition aligns itself with nonsense."

—Brian Hinkley

This is a book for the ordinary person. This is not a book written by an expert, a scholar or a professional writer. For the instruction of the reader, you will not find, in these pages, exhaustive research on the subjects of atheism, religion or the philosophy of life. There are libraries and bookstores full of noble works written by great men and women who are the experts. I have used quotes, in the writing of this book, from some of these great men and women. Where the source is known, I have attempted to reference the quotes, excerpts or passages. Often times, I find many people have the same thoughts, expressed in very much the same language or phraseology. I have found, after writing something, that someone else has already written parallel thoughts. This must be a source of frustration for professional writers, as I am sure they have experienced similar situations.

This book is a collection of my opinions and how I understand Bible writings, religion, etc. However, my opinions are shared by many of the experts. Put another way, I hold many of the same opinions others have expressed before me. However, I suspect that this is not a book experts would care to read. Now that you know what this book is not, let me tell you what this book is and who it is written for.

This is a book about atheism, religion and life, as the title suggests. It is written by a layman, and is about what I experienced while on a journey from religion to atheism.

I became perplexed and curious about the claims being made by the experts. For lack of better terminology, I will simply refer to all the quoted professors, theologians, scientists, authors, biologists, philosophers, etc. as "experts." Some experts may challenge the quality of my research. I am not concerned, as the experts disagree with one another, so it would be quite easy to dismiss a layman's findings. This book is what I know, or think I know. It is what I have experienced, and it is what I have questioned on my journey to atheism.

I explore the question as to whether there is or there is not a God, an Allah, or a Yahweh. I investigate claims of the Bible, and briefly touch on the Koran and the Torah, all books that profess to be the word of their god. My focus, for the most part, is on the Bible and Christianity, as this is what I know most. I examine the claims that there is a heaven and hell. These, along with a host of other assertions, experts will continue to argue. It leaves the rest of us out of the discussion. The majority of ordinary people are left on the sidelines as observers. Why? Because it is impossible to be an expert, on everything, when so many fields of research converge.

To tackle the never-ending quest of searching for truth, the general population relies on experts. We also rely on our parents, teachers and upbringing. (Although one cannot always rely on these for the truth.) With all my warts and imperfections, I attempt to bring to the reader information in a form and style that may prove useful to the novice atheist or those who have begun to question their faith. I concede to the experts the shortcoming of this book. Experts may seek out other scholarly colleagues to test their suppositions, as this book approaches the subject from a different angle.

On a two-week trip to Ukraine in the 1980s, I spent a day with a Ukrainian physicist. He was about forty years old and had never spent a minute outside of Ukraine. He was desperate to know how democracy functioned. It was a day I shall never forget, and all the various subjects we discussed are not for this book. He had a ravenous appetite for knowledge. Of all our conversations, he uttered some words that stuck with me. He said, *"We are all the product of our environment, history and circumstance."* I don't know if he was quoting someone else, but it seemed to summarize all that we as people have come to believe or become as individuals.

If an individual lives in a religious environment, born into a family and society with a history of religiosity, you have become captive to your circumstances. This seems to apply to Christians, Muslims, Jews or any other religion…or non-religion. You cannot change your place of birth or your history (although history is often revised), but what if your environment or your circumstances change? This is what happens to those who question the way things are. It tends to change you. Those who never question anything tend to remain much the same throughout their lives. It is through constant questioning that change occurs, and this includes changes in individuals.

Different situations affect each individual in a most private and personal way. Something might happen at a point in time that triggers the thinking mechanism. Religion, for the most part, discourages people from independent thinking and inhibits any challenge to religious dogma. Atheists, for the most part, encourage you to question and challenge everything. What is it therefore that results in changes in people? It is a change in environment or circumstances that ultimately changes the individual.

Often the change results because the individual acquired new (at least new to them) information about a particular subject. This is what happened in my case.

My journey from religion to atheism is found in this book under the heading **"The Making of an Atheist."** As I say in my story, I came to atheism late in life. I wasn't overly religious, but I was a believer. I tend to think most people who attend church are in the same category. They go along to get along. I suspect that most folks don't believe everything the Bible says or what is preached from the pulpit. However, it is expected to be considered a good person that you should go to church. Many have found that to be good you don't need church or religion in your life.

Why, therefore, this book, written for the layperson by a layperson? After all, there is a flood of books on the market written by the so-called "New Atheists." The books written by the experts are indeed great! In the back pages of this book, I list my favourite resources that led me to my de-conversion. I highly recommend these sources for your reading, research and listening pleasure.

During the process of my de-conversion from religion to atheism, I realized a number of things. The Christian religion talks about how Jesus taught by telling stories or parables. I thought I should tell a few stories, of my own, on how religion has failed the individual and society.

There are two types of stories in this book. There are Bible stories; some of which will be familiar to the reader. Other Bible stories I hope are new to the reader. These are Bible stories that preachers tend to ignore, in total or in part, and do not want their congregation to hear.

My personal comments are interspersed throughout the stories to assist the reader to understand the situation and provide context. The other stories are originals of mine that allow the reader to share the everyday lives of ordinary people as they interface with religion. Sometimes the message is subtle; sometimes the message is blunt. In all, I attempt to leave the reader thinking.

As a professional arbitrator, I decided to write a fictional arbitration on the question of the existence of God and Jesus. I know others have written similar pieces and some of the pro and con arguments cannot help but be repetitious. I have tried to freshen up this debate and package it not precisely in the normal fashion of a decision, taking into consideration my audience. My training did not allow me to stray too much off the rules of evidence, due process and legal procedures codified in a proper arbitration hearing. This might prove to be rather dry reading, unlike some other portions of the book.

I also found new terminology to be confusing. I came across scientific and religious words that made no sense to me. If you don't understand the language of the messenger, how could one ever understand the message? There is a section in this book on words and jargon that may assist you in future reading of the subject.

I realized that relating to people in everyday situations needed to be explained simply rather than by way of a complicated scientific or theological approach that often leaves one dizzy. The Bible, and especially Jesus, spoke in riddles. I try to unravel much of this strange language so ordinary people may relate to the message. The reader will find a liberal use of quotes throughout this book. I believe a succinct quote is often more effective in sending a message than a long dissertation on a subject.

Quotes

"God is the Spirit hovering over the waters of the primordial Earth—Creator of the universe (matter, energy, space, and time), along with other principalities and beings whose primary existence is outside this universe. Someone who lives a 'good' life, but rejects Jesus will be resigned to spend eternity in Hell, whereas someone who commits evil deeds, but accepts Jesus as Lord and Saviour immediately before execution for murder will go to heaven. It is true that God is not fair. Those who call for fairness will get the fairness of God's justice. As for me, I prefer God's mercy over God's justice. It is through God's outrageous love and mercy toward those who humble themselves that we can become sons and daughters of God. Glory be to His Name!"

—**Richard L. Deem**; received his Bachelor of Science degree in biological sciences at the University of Southern California. He received his Master of Science degree in microbiology from California State University, Los Angeles, and has been working in basic science research since 1976. He has authored and co-authored a number of studies, included several areas of molecular biology and genetics, immunology, inflammatory bowel disease, natural killer cells and infectious diseases. In addition, he has presented his work at a number of national and international scientific meetings.

~

"I have never, in all my life, not for one moment, been tempted toward religion of any kind. The fact is that I feel no spiritual void. I have my philosophy of life, which does not include any aspect of the supernatural and which I find totally satisfying. I am, in short, a rationalist and believe only that which reason tells me is so."

—Isaac Asimov; Isaac Asimov was a Russian-born American author, a professor of biochemistry and a highly successful writer, best known for his works of science fiction and for his popular science books. Professor Asimov is generally considered the most prolific writer of all time, having written or edited more than five hundred books and an estimated ninety thousand letters and postcards. He has works published in nine of the ten major categories of the Dewey Decimal System (lacking only an entry in the 100s class of Philosophy).

~

"The God of the Old Testament is arguably the most unpleasant character in all fiction: jealous and proud of it; a petty, unjust, unforgiving control-freak; a vindictive, bloodthirsty ethnic cleanser; a misogynistic, homophobic, racist, infanticidal, genocidal, filicidal, pestilential, megalomaniacal, sadomasochistic, capriciously malevolent bully."

—Richard Dawkins; Clinton Richard Dawkins, DSc, FRS, FRSL is an ethnologist, evolutionary biologist and writer. He is an emeritus fellow of New College, Oxford, and was the University of Oxford's Professor for Public Understanding of Science from 1995 until 2008. Author of *The God Delusion.*

~

To My Christian Friends

With help from Bobby C. of *No Religion Required* podcast

I know facts that dispute the Bible's claims can be seen as offensive to you, but I hope you will read some of what I've written and give it some serious thought. I spent 60 plus years as a Christian. I was not a Bible-thumping Christian. In fact, I seldom read the Bible. It wasn't until I really started reading the Bible that I became an atheist. Yes, I became an atheist after reading the Bible.

I firmly believe that the reason Christians have an issue with atheism is because they don't understand it. I was one of those people in the past. Atheism to me was something bad. Atheists were seen as devil worshipers and were to be avoided at all costs! Then I learned late in life there is no devil and there is no god.

I want to help you understand what it means to be an atheist with the hopes that it will help you see atheists through a different lens.

I would venture to say that as a Christian you do not believe in the Hindu god, Krishna, or in the Muslim god, Allah. However, to the people who follow these religions, you are considered an atheist. To be an atheist does not mean to be against God, as it is often taught in church. Atheism is a non-belief in a god or gods. My lack of belief in a Christian god or any other god is no different from your lack of belief in Krishna, Allah, Buddha, Mohammed, or any other god outside of Christianity.

There are good and bad atheists, just as there are good and bad believers in religion. Those who act inhumanly really bother me. These people and their actions make those who want the very best for humanity look bad in the eyes of the world. Most atheists also consider themselves humanists, who fully believe that every person deserves to be treated equally. I am one of those people. Every person deserves equal rights regardless of their sex, race, religion or non-religion and sexual orientation.

If you have read this far and decide to read some stories of my interpretation of the Bible, you just may see things a little differently. You may find things you didn't know were in the Bible. I didn't know they were there until I started reading the Bible. I was always taught about the good things Jesus was supposed to have done.

In Sunday school or church, the pastor focused on the passages that taught kindness, generosity and compassion. This is what I thought the Bible was about. When I started noticing the terrible murders, rapes and killing of innocent little children…all in the name of God, it was upsetting.

My initial impression was that this was not true. The more I read the Bible, the more I became disgusted with this so-called loving god. When I asked various church leaders and religious folks about these verses, no one really had good answers. They seemed to want to avoid discussing these things. The most common answer I was given is that God does not expect me to question what was written but to only accept it on faith. This did not work for me, and it left me with even more questions. With none of my questions answered, I started looking outside of Christianity for answers. I did a little study of Islam, Buddhism, Hinduism, Judaism, Jainism and other religions and found that they were basically the same. This left me feeling uneasy.

I finally came to the realization that any god, and in my opinion, all such gods, were man-made. That there was no invisible man in the sky watching everything I do, listening to everything I say and think. I realized I could see no god. I could feel no god. I could hear no god. No god ever talked to me. When I used to pray to God, he never answered my prayers. I could smell no god, and I could certainly taste no god, unlike the Catholics, who perform some kind of cannibalistic ritual of eating the body of Christ and drinking his blood. I was finally free of any god and any religion. It felt wonderful!

I encourage you to read my Bible stories and of course the other parts of my book. I know some parts of this book will make you feel uncomfortable, and I will not apologize for that. I ask you to consider what I've written and research the scriptures for yourself. Perhaps, after some time, you may think differently about this god that you pray to.

~

The Making of an Atheist

"When I was a kid I had an imaginary friend and I used to think that he went everywhere with me, and that I could talk to him and that he could hear me, and that he could grant me wishes and stuff. And then I grew up, and I stopped going to church." **—Jimmy Carr, Comedian**

The Making of an Atheist

Why did it take me so long? This is a question that I ask myself now that I am retired and have the time to think about such things. Freedom from religion, and an invisible god, came to me rather late in my life. Why now? I decided to trace incidents in my life that led me to atheism. Here is my story.

THE EARLY YEARS

Our family was poor and on the low end of the working class. Even though we were poor, I never thought much about poverty, as it seemed most everyone was in the same boat. The real poor people were those on relief. That's what we called welfare in those days.

My mother was religious of sorts; not fanatical, but a believer. It was handed down to her from her grandmother. My mother was raised by her grandmother, as her mother was incapable. But that's another story. At the time I did not pay much attention to my mother's religious comments. They just lacked meaning to me. My father was not religious at all. He had nothing good to say about Jews, Catholics or any religion. My father's comments seemed to have more substance than my mother's, but both my parents provided very little in the way of answering questions that I had about religion and God. Ironically, my grandfather (on my father's side) was a devout Jehovah's Witness. My grandfather actually built two separate churches entirely by himself. He was quite a good carpenter, just like Jesus was supposed to be. Unfortunately, I have never seen anything built by Jesus. I guess I will just have to take it on faith that Jesus was indeed a carpenter. The Jehovah's Witnesses seem to have different names for things. They call their churches Kingdom Halls.

I remember my mother watching Oral Roberts on television. She was totally enthralled, enchanted and spellbound by his evangelical fervour. I thought it was hilarious. I would watch the television and these religious antics for pure entertainment. I loved the part when Oral Roberts would hit people on the head, knock them to the floor, and heal them of their illness. I would roll on the floor with laughter and run through the house yelling *"I've been healed. I've been healed."* I have three brothers, all older than me. Whenever one of them did or said something bad, one of the brothers would smack the other on the head and say, *"Heal thyself. Cast the devil out."* This little game was a constant source of amusement.

All my brothers, at various times, attended church and Sunday school, but it was more for the recreational pursuits. It was the First United Church that provided the community with basketball, crafts and all sorts of other activities. It kept us out of trouble. For this, I will always be grateful. I had a lot of good times with sports activities and making things in the woodworking room. I attended Sunday school out of appreciation for these activities. I guess it was my way of saying thank you to the church for all the good things they provided.

Sunday school provided some information about the Bible. It was almost always about Jesus. Jesus was portrayed as nice, kind and gentle, especially towards children. We were never told of an angry Jesus…but for some reason, I was really scared of God. And yet, I can never remember hearing anything about bloodshed, wars, slaughter, rape, incest, genocide, etc. The closest to anything violent was the story of David and Goliath. But this was presented as the nice, meek, little David fighting the good fight against the big, nasty, bad Goliath.

It wasn't until fifty years later that I learned what an efficient killing machine this David fellow had become.

All the other stories were about good deeds and miracles performed by Jesus. The miracles seemed like a fantasy to me. Just like Oral Roberts. My favourite story was the one about the "Good Samaritan." That stuck with me more than all the rest. It seemed real and possible and didn't involve some kind of miracle.

A favourite pastime of the neighbourhood children was to follow the Salvation Army marching bands. In those days, the Salvation Army (we called them the **Salivation** Army) had their brass band march through the neighbourhood streets. They would stop at a corner or a park to play more songs and sing hymns. The Captain (they weren't called preachers) would give a sermon, followed by a public collection by the onlookers in attendance.

For me and the other children, this was entertainment and great fun! We never knew when they would march, but you sure could hear them. They were loud! I loved the sound of the tuba most of all. When we heard the music, kids (it seemed it was mostly kids, but some adults too) would charge out of their homes and follow the band. It was always a sight to behold. This loud marching band with men and women, all in nicely pressed uniforms, was followed by a horde of people behind them. It looked sort of like a Pied Piper parade.

One day I heard the band playing and jumped so fast I ran right into the door. The door was stuck, and I couldn't open it. My mother was yelling for me to wait. I was all excited and was about to scoot out the door. She said, *"Here is a dime for the collection."* You see, the Salvation Army was special to our entire family.

My family had some tough times, and the Army came through for us. Even my father was thankful for their help. To this day, every one of my brothers gives money to the Salvation Army. I do, too, especially at Christmas. Regardless of my non-religiosity, I will never forget the good they did in the community and continue to do today.

The neighbourhood kids did something that I'm sure the members of the Salvation Army did not really appreciate. It was done in a rather mocking tone. But the Army members were too polite to admonish us. The kids would follow behind, and invariably all of us in unison would chant — some called it singing — the following:

> "Salvation Army save my soul,
> Send me up to heaven in a sugar bowl.
> If the sugar bowl cracks and down I fall,
> Save me from the fire of the Devil's hole."

Being a kid, I was not allowed alone in some parts of the First United Church building. It was a huge, dominant building, with its tennis courts and landscaped area — it took up an entire city block. It really was impressive. I had seen the church assembly area, the gymnasium and the crafts room. The Sunday school room reminded me of a kindergarten classroom. But I had never seen the rest of the church.

One day, during the week when I was off school, I went over to watch the adults play tennis. The fenced-in tennis courts were restricted for special people, called VIPs. It was many years before I found out what was meant by "VIPs." The doors to the church were often locked, but not always. This day I watched someone enter the side door of the church. When the door closed, I went over and opened the door.

I cautiously entered. It all seemed so strange and quiet. Long corridors with big oak doors and ornate wood carvings were everywhere. What impressed me the most was the plush red carpeting. When you walked on it not a sound was made, but sometimes the stairs would creak.

Large paintings of the portraits of past ministers hung along the corridors. All of them were males. They were dressed in fancy gold-lined gowns, some with fur collars. Red and white seemed to be popular colours, with some black. Most of them did not look very happy.

As I skulked along the corridor, I felt as though every one of these stern-looking ministers was staring down at me. It was as though their eyes were following me. I felt that any moment I would be struck by the wrath of God. It was eerie. It felt creepy. I then heard voices behind a door. My little heart started to thump so hard I thought I was going to faint. I ran out of the church as fast as my little legs would carry me. I never did that again. I suppose that was the only time I felt like I got close to God…and it scared the hell out of me.

A few years later, the church burned down. In those days, it seemed a lot of churches burned to the ground. I thought it was odd that so many churches would catch fire. Why wouldn't God protect his house of worship? I made a strange connection in my mind's eye that had no rhyme or reason. Every Victoria Day in Canada (the kids called it Firecracker Day), a fireworks display of a burning schoolhouse was set off.

I always thought it should be a church burning, as I remember more fires at churches than at schoolhouses.

A few more years had passed when I first heard the word "atheist." It started to make me think. I believe I had heard the word before, but it didn't mean a thing to me. From what I could tell, an atheist was not a good person. Why they were not good people, I didn't know. One day my father just casually mentioned he was an atheist. Did this mean my father was some kind of bad person? I was confused. What the heck is an atheist?

Nothing was ever explained to me about atheism. I was shown how to chop wood, ride a bike, bait a fishing hook, take out the ashes, drive a car, and much more, but religion was something that was in that little black Bible that my mother inherited from her grandmother.

One day I opened my mother's Bible. Maybe I was ten years old. I tried reading the Bible. What the heck is this? What kind of language is this? It looked like English, but the words didn't make sense to me. Thee and thou, smiting, begat, people living four hundred years, and someone else living two and thirty years, and people are to know Him, and others divided Himself among them. I was totally confused. I couldn't make sense of it. For the next fifty years, I could never remember reading the Bible again. Ironically, now that I am an atheist, the Bible is a constant source of amusement and entertainment. I have never read a novel with so much blood and guts, killings, rapes, wars, hatred, jealousy, greed, animosity, women hating, children suffering, disease and wicked weather patterns — all of this...and so much more, commanded by or carried out by this so-called loving God. If this is love, I'd hate to get this guy really angry at me.

On my sixteenth birthday, as a birthday present, my father told me it was time for me to get out and earn my own living. He was not going to keep me any longer.

All of my brothers finished their schooling by age sixteen or before. I was in high school at the time and had dreams of becoming a teacher. Those dreams were dashed.

I held this against my father for many years. Over time I realized something. My father came from England, and this was common among the English. At sixteen you are a man. You stand on your own two feet and support yourself. So that's exactly what I did. I left home, got a job, and I have been working ever since.

THE MIDDLE YEARS

As the years passed, my main focus was on earning a living and raising a family. During the next fifty years I held a myriad of jobs. I was a spray painter, meat packer, truck driver, various factory labour jobs, and stock controller, just to name a few. At one point I worked a full-time job during the day and two part-time jobs. I delivered Chinese food and drove taxi on the weekends and in the evenings.

I got married, had two kids, got divorced, and married again. In between all of this, I continued to take night school courses at community colleges, university and adult special interest courses.

My big break in academic advancement occurred when I became heavily involved in the United Steelworkers of America. These were heady days for the Steelworkers. They had considerable strength and bargaining power. I attended every educational course that the union and the Canadian Labour Congress offered. These included subjects on political science, sociology, collective bargaining, negotiations, leadership training, psychology and human relations, grievance handling and dispute resolution.

My involvement in the union was all-consuming. I negotiated contracts, attended arbitrations, and took a year leave from my regular job to work full-time with the union on organizing companies.

Along with the week-long or weekend seminars, I also completed a six-month correspondence course. This qualified me to submit an application for a scholarship to attend a two-month residential training and education program at the Canadian Labour College located at the University of Montreal. I made an application and succeeded in winning a scholarship in a competition among several of my peers.

The Labour College experience led me to elected public office and to my current field of arbitration and mediation. When I completed Labour College, I returned to the union for a short time before running for my local City Council. I was successful and was re-elected for many terms, serving a total of fifteen years as an Alderman and Councillor. I also ran unsuccessfully for the Provincial Legislature and the Mayoralty. I volunteered my services for several years with the Buffalo Better Business Bureau – Conflict Resolution Centre. This allowed me to diversify my training in the field of conflict resolution methods. For the past twenty-two years I have conducted a private conflict resolution service focused mainly on arbitration and mediation.

All during this time, church and religion was not a priority. The only time I attended church was for reasons of community and charity events, weddings or funerals, or local politics. I never questioned the existence of Jesus or a deity. I didn't challenge the folks who believed in the Bible. To get along, I just went along.

At one point, and I can't remember when, I did give a few seconds reflection about the hypocrisy of religion. From my way of thinking, I always believed many religious folks were hypocrites. On the other hand, I have met good people who are strong believers. Nonetheless, I always thought religion itself was full of hypocrisy and silliness. I still did not give atheism a moment's thought.

This feeling of hypocrisy came riveting home to me at a church event. I was in my early forties when I attended this church service as part of my duties as an Alderman. After the service, some of the congregation gathered in the basement for a social. The church's Women's Auxiliary had prepared sandwiches, pastries and refreshments.

What I subsequently overheard and observed has always bothered me. We had just come from a sermon about the *"Good Samaritan."* The minister had gone on about our obligation to the needy in our community, and the church was in the midst of raising funds for the local food bank.

You will need to visualize this social setting in your mind's eye. All the folks in the room were well dressed. Most were long-time members of the congregation. Almost all the men wore suits and ties. The women wore lovely flowered dresses, with plenty of jewellery adorning their necks, ears and fingers.

While I was filling my plate with goodies, I overheard the conversation of two matronly ladies of the church. They both seemed to delight in gossip. I thought to myself, *"This kind of talk is not very Christian-like."* I consciously tried to ignore their conversation, as I would rather not know of such things. But then my ears perked up when one lady said, *"Look at that — isn't that disgusting."*

She was referring to a man in the corner of the room. He was all alone, not really bothering anyone. His clothes were ragged, and he was unkempt. His hands were dirty, and his black fingernails stood out against the white-bread sandwich he held in his hand.

He was also stuffing food into his pockets. One of the women motioned for the minister's attention. The minister was roving around the room greeting folks with this big smile on his face. The woman raised her disgust with the minister. The minister went into the kitchen and talked to one of the women from the auxiliary.

I remembered seeing this fellow in the church service. He had sat right at the back pew in the end seat. He was a sad-looking chap who had, no doubt, experienced a hard life. This was no surprise to me. After all, many of my constituents were in the same dire circumstances.

As best as I could, I tried to remain inconspicuous and I slowly made my way over to the kitchen area. I was afraid some kind of scene was going to occur. The lady from the kitchen approached the man. The man started to shake and immediately said, *"I didn't mean to take the sandwiches."* The lady, in a very soft voice, said, *"That's all right; you keep the food. Come with me into the kitchen, and you can have all you want. In fact, when the social is over, I'll give you a package that you can take home."*

Obviously, the minister did not want to offend these two long-standing members of the congregation, so he tried to delicately defuse the situation. There are certain things, certain times, when an event takes place that is burned into your memory. It is like a cow being branded with a hot iron. It is embedded in your consciousness for the rest of your life. I will never forget this incident.

I thought to myself, what hypocrisy! I also thought to myself how nice the lady from the auxiliary behaved. I simply chalked it up as some folks know the right thing to do and others never will — religion or no religion.

As the years passed, religion played a very small part in my life. I guess I still believed there was some kind of god. And this Jesus fellow — I kind of liked what he had to say. Had I read the Bible by this time? No, I had not.

THE SENIOR YEARS

I am now sixty-nine and semi-retired. I have the luxury of having more time to read, study and pursue matters of interest. I missed having a dog. I always had dogs when I was young. Unfortunately, for most of my adult life a dog did not fit my lifestyle. I told my wife, twenty years before I eased into my somewhat retired state, that I would get a Basenji dog. She said, *"What the heck is a Basenji?"* Well, this is a long story. Suffice it to say that this little dog has brought more joy, happiness and laughter into our lives than words can express. He also scared us to tears when we thought we were going to lose him to a sudden illness, but he has since recovered.

When I reached sixty-one years old, I was fairly contented with my life, my wife and my little dog…and no religion. But I was still not one of those nasty atheists.

Over time a few things began to happen. First there was this television news story about a bunch of atheists in London, England, who were advertising various slogans. The news coverage described the atheists as radicals, and overall the story was quite negative towards them. This started me thinking. I can't remember the slogans they used, but it made me think. The thinking did not last very long, and I continued on with the rest of my life.

Maybe a year or so later, I saw another television news story. The United States was experiencing a lot of tornadoes and hurricanes and several destructive storms. Many folks were killed or left homeless due to the devastation. This little elderly woman was standing all alone in the middle of mass destruction all around her. Not a single building was left standing. All her neighbours were wiped out. Some of them killed. And she was standing there, in front of the TV camera, thanking God because she was spared and was still alive. I thought to myself, huh? What the heck is this lady talking about? An act of God just finished destroying people's lives and property. God just finished causing untold misery to many folks, who I am sure were quite religious and decent people. How in the world could anyone be thanking God for this act? The truth is that God had nothing to do with the devastation or for saving the little old lady. It was all the work of nature.

I watched a PBS show when Bill Moyers was interviewing an author of several books; her name, Susan Jacoby. Listening to her talk, I thought, well, this is an intelligent woman. I started to read her books: *Never Say Die: The Myth and Marketing of the New Old Age*; *The Age of American Unreason*; and *The Great Agnostic: Robert Ingersoll and American Freethought*. These books, her website and her other writings led me to a whole host of books and a wealth of information. I read books by Richard Dawkins, Christopher Hitchens, Sam Harris and a long list of other authors. Of course, Richard Dawkins' *God Delusion* was the clincher. I suppose it was my epiphany.

I finally realized that I WAS an atheist. What I really did not know was the amount of information available on atheism. I had no idea there were organized groups of atheists. I thought atheists were these lone, solitary, non-conformist individuals.

Where was this information all my life? I was astonished to find so many atheist organizations. Why hadn't I heard of them before? The Internet and various websites flourish with information. I started to read the Bible and learned just how monstrous the invisible man in the sky really is. It is unbelievable the amount of cruelty and lust for violence this whole religion-god thing has foisted upon humanity.

I thought, how stupid, how naïve, how dumb could I be? But then there are so many highly educated, very smart and intelligent leaders in this world who are totally religious, believe in angels, miracles and the resurrection. Maybe I'm not the dumb one after all.

I had the impression that atheists were some kind of warped, nasty, bad people. After checking various websites, listening to various podcasts and reading a ton of superb books and articles, I find that most atheists are nice, good and moral people. However, I shudder with bewilderment when I watch and hear the pixilated* rants of religious fanatics. So I decided to join at least one of the many atheist organizations. I chose the Freedom from Religion Foundation. Dan Barker and Annie Laurie Gaylor, co-presidents of the FFRF, seem like very nice people, not at all what an atheist is supposed to be.

At sixty-nine years old, it is astonishing that I have lived such a sheltered life. Now I spend much of my time reading the manic and vile history of religion. I take great pleasure in reading the writings of Robert Green Ingersoll – The Great Agnostic (August 11, 1833 – July 21, 1899). What a remarkable human being this man must have been. He has become my latest hero. His intelligence, compassion, vision, unshakable grasp of reality, common sense and master of the English language is nothing short of genius.

His life-changing speeches and writings can be read, watched or listened to at the following website: http://www.robertgreeningersoll.org

This brings me back to my original question. Why did it take me so long?

*Pixelated vs. pixilated

Though *pixelated* is the standard spelling of the word meaning *rendered with visible pixels,* there's a good reason that spell-check does not catch *pixilated*.

Pixilated is an old, seldom-used Americanism dating from the middle of the nineteenth century and peaking (in this use) in the middle twentieth century. It meant (1) *crazed, bewildered, or whimsical*, or (2) *intoxicated*.

Pixilated derives from the noun *pixie*, denoting a mythical, mischievous creature. One who is pixilated is under the sway of a figurative pixie or behaving in a pixie-like manner. The word's exact origins are not known.

Whether anyone still uses *pixilated* this way is difficult to say. In historical Google News searches, most of the instances of *pixilated* used this way are from the 1930s and '40s, with only a few scattered examples from after 1950.

Time was, anyone we thought was pixilated was merely called nuts, screwy, or wacky.

~

Bible Stories

The Killing God

"'I will sweep away everything in all your land,' says the LORD. 'I will sweep away both people and animals alike. Even the birds of the air and the fish in the sea will die. I will reduce the wicked to heaps of rubble, along with the rest of humanity,' says the LORD. 'I will crush Judah and Jerusalem with my fist and destroy every last trace of their Baal worship. I will put an end to all the idolatrous priests, so that even the memory of them will disappear. For they go up to their roofs and bow to the sun, moon, and stars. They claim to follow the LORD, but then they worship Molech, too. So now I will destroy them! And I will destroy those who used to worship me but now no longer do. They no longer ask for the LORD's guidance or seek my blessings.'"

—Zephaniah 1:2-6 (NLT)

Joshua and the Slaughter of the Canaanites

Chorus
Joshua fought the battle of Jericho, Jericho, Jericho
Joshua fought the battle of Jericho
and the walls came a-tumbling down

You may talk about your men of Gideon
You may talk about the men of Saul
But there's none like good old Joshua
at the battle of Jericho (that mornin')

Nice song, eh? Wait till you read the story.

The Slaughter of the Canaanites

WHAT? One day, the God of Abraham decided it was once again time to wipe out some more of his creations. The Bible records there is this god that gets off on killing sprees. The god of the Bible says: ***"Thou shall not kill."*** However, this same god delivers enormous pain and suffering as he undertakes massive killings. He commits these crimes either by his own hand or by giving commands to his earthly subordinates. It is said, your deeds expose your character and this god is quite a character. He operates under the doctrine. Do as I say, not as I do.

This god knows how to persuade his believers to commit murder, rape and the slaughter of many innocents. After all, he is on this seemingly endless pursuit to purify humanity. Remember the big flood! Apparently it failed to wash away the sinners. But, he kept on trying. This time, rather than killing all of earthly humanity, including little babies, the unborn and all living creatures, except for Noah and his virtuous family, he decides to kill only a few thousand Canaanites. These poor folks were all descendants of Mr. Noah, the virtuous one. Actually, Noah apparently wasn't all that virtuous to begin with. Makes you question this god's ability to judge character.

WHO are the Canaanites? The Canaanites are named for their ancestor called Canaan, the son of Ham and grandson of Noah. I'm not kidding — the grandson of Noah. There is a subplot to this rather complicated story. Ham, the son of Noah, walked into Noah's tent one evening. The old man liked his wine and would often imbibe to excess. Noah fell into one of his drunken stupors and fell fast asleep — naked. What was poor Ham's sin? Well, he saw the old man in his birthday suit. For this, Noah cursed Ham.

But it wasn't Ham alone that suffered from this curse. In some convoluted reasoning, by being the fourth son, so should it be that the fourth son of Ham, that being Canaan, should also be cursed. Go figure?

I apologize for straying from the main story, so let's get back to the main plot. After old Noah dried himself out, there was a lot of begatting to do to repopulate the world.

In those days, the whole world was Jews. But this is somewhat debatable. Maybe they were just called Israelites or Hebrews. Is there a difference? If they were Jews, then they/we are all Jews. At any rate, they were all, apparently, God's chosen children. As the population grew, the people split into different tribes. You can call them nations…that sounds better. Nations need leaders. Leaders always seem to want to carve out their own land. So it was in the days of Abraham. Well, all of Noah's offspring eventually went their separate ways and split up into various nations.

WHERE did these various nations settle? The Bible world was apparently a much smaller place in those days. It seemed they were all squished together in the lands around the Mediterranean Sea. They apparently divided up the land and gave them names like Israel, Judah, Mohad and so on. It seems they could not find their way further into Africa, the rest of Europe or Asia, so they fought over this small part of the world…just like they continue to do today. Certainly, this god would not take sides in disputes among his own children.

It is fascinating how this god chose only this small part of the world to deliver his message. Somehow the millions of Chinese (and other Asians), the millions of Indians and all the rest of the world's inhabitants were forgotten.

Back to his real children. What should you do when your
children get into spats among themselves? But, of course;
you should kill the delinquents. That is what this loving
god ordered. It is obvious this god was not aware of the
modern psychology of raising children. His ill-behaved
Canaanite children were not the only ones to be slaughtered.
This god has quite a record of being drunk with blood. You
really don't want to piss this guy off. He has one long
memory and many creative ways to seek revenge.

WHY kill the Canaanites? I cannot provide a rational
answer to this question. I searched out an expert in
theology. There are many experts to choose from. You do
need a highly educated, extremely smart and intelligent
person to answer this question. I settled on Dr. William
Lane Craig. He is a Research Professor of Philosophy at
Talbot School of Theology Houston Baptist University.
More on this smart, intelligent and educated expert at
http://www.reasonablefaith.org/slaughter-of-the-canaanites.

Here is a reprint of a question put to Dr. Craig by one
reader of his website (website now changed):

*"In the forums, there has been some good questions
raised on the issue of God commanding the Jews to
commit 'genocide' on the people in the promise land. As
you have pointed out in some of your written work that
this act does not fit with the Western concept of God being
the big sugar daddy in the sky. Now we can certainly find
justification for those people coming under God's
judgement because of their sins, idolatry, sacrificing their
children, etc... But a harder question is the killing of the
children and infants. The children and young, along with
the infants; are innocent of the sins that their society has
committed. How do we reconcile this command of God to
kill the children with the concept of his holiness?"*

Answer: Dr. Craig is long-winded, and I am being charitable. Dr. Craig must follow the old idiom of why use a few words when a few thousand will do. Feel free to rummage through Dr. Craig's answer at the above website. I have filtered his response and can only conclude that the following quote, from his reply, is the best way to summarize his answer.

"On divine command theory, then, God has the right to command an act, which, in the absence of a divine command, would have been sin, but which is now morally obligatory in virtue of that command."

For thousands of years, deluded people have invoked religion or the name of a god for the commission of acts against humanity. Every era has its own Charles Manson, Jimmy Jones, and David Koresh, along with a whole host of insane and deluded believers who justify their orders and behaviour as commanded by a god. I have concluded those who claim to talk to a god and, in turn, that this god talks to them are seriously mentally ill.

Back to the story. By now, the 950-year-old Noah finally expired. Can you believe it; 950 years! No wonder he took to the bottle. After years of the nagging he suffered from the invisible man in the sky, who could blame the old-timer for taking a few drinks? If all of the preceding seems a stretch, buckle your seat belts. What follows is the stuff of ultimate horror. It makes the snuff movie *Cannibal Holocaust* seem like a children's story. The Biblical account describes the Israelites as being led by Joshua and crossing the Jordan into Canaan where they laid siege to the city of Jericho. OK, let us pause to find out who is this Joshua fellow. According to the Bible, he became the leader of the Israelite tribes after the death of Moses.

He was the son of Nun of the tribe of Ephraim. I'm sure that makes it as clear as mud for you.

He was one of the twelve spies of Israel sent by Moses to explore the land of Canaan. I do not know why they needed to sneak around when, after all, they already had the big spy in the sky on their team. After the death of Moses, Joshua led the Israelite tribes in the conquest of Canaan and allocated the land to the tribes. With help from the Almighty, he had quite a future as God's hitman. Joshua is recorded as one of the most bloodthirsty, proficient destroyers of human life. He is praised in the pages of the Bible. Hitler would have been proud of Joshua's military might.

Although Joshua was a real killer, I must hand it to him and the help he received from his skyward friend, when together they conspired to have the sun stand still for an entire twenty-four hours. Actually, if the ancient writers of this fantasy knew anything about the rotation of the earth, they wouldn't have written such a ridiculous passage. But this was yet another of a long list of killing sprees. I'll leave the slaughter of the Amorites and get back to these nasty Canaanites.

Apparently the Supreme Moralist (god) did not like the behaviour of the Canaanites, especially the sexual behaviour. God spoke to Joshua telling him to march around the city once every day for six days with seven priests carrying ram's horns. On the seventh day they were to march around the city seven times and the priests were to blow their ram's horns. And Joshua ordered the people to shout. The walls of the Jericho collapsed, (It must have been one hell of a noise) and the Israelites were able to charge straight into the city. The city was completely destroyed, and every man, woman, child and animal was killed by Joshua's army.

All this slaughtering mayhem was ordered by God's command. Only Rahab and her family were spared, because she had conspired and hid two spies sent by Joshua. Espionage apparently flourished in those days, too.

It is time to pause once more to find out who is this one called Rahab. Rahab was one of those unexpected characters in the Bible. Even though she made her living as a prostitute, she was selected to be spared. This is another contradiction of the Bible's interesting rationalization of ethics and morals. Rahab was spared the thrust of the sword, unlike the innocent little babies suckling on their mother's breasts. The innocent little babies were slain with impunity. They never had the opportunity to grow up to be prostitutes and engage in espionage. The optics of infants with their heads severed from their little bodies, the blood and guts, the blood-curdling screams, and the horrors of a god-created hell on earth could only be described as genocide.

After this bloodletting, Joshua burned the remains of the city and cursed any man who tried to rebuild the city of Jericho. Any such action would result in the slaying of his first-born son. Notice that the writers of the Bible never say their first-born daughter. Women, you see, in this god's eye, were just slightly better than the beasts of burden. Although, if a man had to choose between his donkey and his wife, he may have chosen the donkey.

Yet, one can find these cute religious Bible stories taught by Sunday school teachers. Children, too young to understand context, are told how lovely it was that the walls of Jericho came tumbling down. Yes, I remember it well. They even put the story to verse and song. How the nice Mr. Joshua took care of those nasty Canaanites.

Contrary to what some Bible believers claim, the Canaanites were not the absolute worst specimens of humanity that ever existed — or the worst that existed in the ancient Near East. Who is to say that these accounts are just like that of any army in history attacking another people in the name of a god? So maybe Joshua was not so bad as far as history's recordings of mass murderers. You could say he was just an ordinary bloodthirsty murderer operating in the name of a god. Now, all those in favour of genocide, please raise your hands!

Doesn't this story give you a nice, warm, fuzzy feeling about this so-called loving, compassionate and caring god? Ah, the morality of the Bible. Makes you want to rush out and do the God of Abraham's bidding...doesn't it?

All together now, let's sing!

Joshua fought the battle of Jericho, Jericho, Jericho
Joshua fought the battle of Jericho
and the walls came a-tumbling down.

~

The Violent Levite

The Violent Levite Sparks Civil War

The book of Judges has it all: sex (of all kinds), some of the most gruesome violence, lies, deceit, incest, sacrifices, rapes, suicide — anyway, you get the picture. Speaking of pictures, this, one of the smaller books of the Bible, would make a blockbuster Hollywood movie; what, with so much blood and guts and all.

One could start almost anywhere in Judges, and one would find insane violence. In fact, the talk of bloodlust begins right at the first verse of Judges. **Judges 1:** Now after the death of Joshua it came to pass that the children of Israel asked the LORD, saying, *"Who shall be first to go up for us against the Canaanites to fight against them?"*

Let me say, these Israelites just couldn't wait to get into a good fight and keep on killing. And this is after, supposedly, being told by Abraham, Isaac, Jacob, Moses and Joshua how to behave. (**Pause:** This group of five lived by the saying *"Do as I say, not as I do"...just like God.*) Despite what the big five had to say, these sons and daughters of the chosen people continued to sin, sin, sin and break every one of the Ten Commandments, and a whole lot more. One would think that after four hundred years of bondage, another forty years in the desert with no real food to eat, and a host of rules and admonishment by the big guy himself, that even the dumbest of the dumb would get the message. Any one of the stories of the killings in the book of Judges makes for incredible reading. Most of it is completely bizarre. It's no wonder you never hear pious preachers tell these stories on Sunday in church. They are just too much for any decent human being to stomach. At the risk of making you puke, you are given fair warning about the dangers of reading the following Bible story.

The Violent Levite (Judges 19-21). I have chosen this story not because it is necessarily the worst in the Bible but because it is one of the stories seldom told. These three chapters are simply hideous! In the closing pages of Judges, there is repulsive wife abuse, blatant homosexuality, unconscionable gang rape leading to murder, injustice, brother killing brother, and kidnapping…just to get warmed up. It is curious to note that a phrase keeps appearing in these chapters: **"Now it came about in those days, when there was no king in Israel..."** The reader is continually reminded of this. It's as though all the bad behaviour of the great unwashed was as a consequence of not having a king. Go figure?

Let's get on with the story of this Levite fellow. He is living temporarily in the hill country of Ephraim. He seems to be unemployed or displaced. He is not at Israel's legitimate place of worship, Shiloh (see 18:31). He has acquired a concubine from Bethlehem. Now in those days, a concubine was used interchangeably with the term "wife." It gets a bit confusing. A concubine is also a wife, but a wife is above the status of a concubine, so a wife is not really a concubine, and a concubine not really a wife. A concubine could rise to the level of wife, but then again in those days a wife was probably not as valuable as a donkey. Forget it. Let us continue. This concubine, aka wife, is sexually unfaithful and runs home to her father in Bethlehem for protection. She is gone for four months and her husband misses her; so he travels to Bethlehem, forgives her, and reconciles. (**Pause:** Remember this for later, as his forgiveness is fleeting).

He (the no-name Levite) and his father-in-law discover they enjoy each other's company and spend five days eating, drinking, and being merry.

Little did the Levite realize that he really has nothing to be happy about because tragedy is stalking his marriage. Finally, after five days the couple decides to leave. As they journey, the Levite's servant (where the hell did his servant come from?) asks to spend the night at Jebus (Jerusalem).

(**Pause:** I find when reading the Bible, people appear out of nowhere, then disappear never to be heard of again. Some people, all they have is a name, no history, no connection to anyone, no title, just a name. Some folks, like this Levite, don't even have a name. Go figure?)

Back to the story. Since Jebus is not an Israelite town at the moment, the Levite wants to press on until they are in Israelite territory. So they travel another four miles until they arrive at Gibeah — a town in Benjamite territory.

(**Pause:** What is Benjamite territory? It is an area occupied by one of the twelve tribes of Israel. The tribe started with a man, a patriarch by the name of Benjamin. He was the least-born son of Jacob, born last of all his twelve sons. He was the only son that was born in Palestine. All the other sons (and all the daughters, as far as we know) were born in Mesopotamia in the area adjacent to or in association with Babylon. He was also the son of Jacob. Jacob was well over one hundred years of age when Benjamin was born. The record of Benjamin's birth is in Genesis chapter 35. Don't forget now, these are among God's chosen people.)

Back to the story. The travellers arrive at Gibeah in the darkness and come into the town square, where they expect to be greeted and offered hospitality. Finally, an elderly fellow passes by who is returning from the fields. He is not a Benjamite; his home is in the hill country of Ephraim, but he is living temporarily in Gibeah.

When the old man sees the weary travellers, he invites them to his house for the night, insisting that he provide food for them. (Well, that was very Christian of the old fellow. Oh, pardon me, there were no Christians yet. This old guy must have been ahead of his time.)

After they have just finished eating, the men of the city come to the door and insist that the old man send out the Levite so that they can sexually assault him. The men of Gibeah turn out to be as wicked as the heathen around them! (Pause: Hey, where have I heard of this scene before? Wasn't there a fellow named Lot way back in Genesis 19 who was confronted by a whole bunch of sex-craved homosexuals? They, too, wanted a couple of men turned over to the townsmen in order to have sex with them. It seems God must have loved homosexuals, as he sure made a lot of them back in those days.)

Maybe things turned out a little better in this scene. Let's see. **"Then the old man, the owner of the house, went out to them and said to them, 'No, my fellows, please do not act so wickedly; since this man has come into my house, do not commit this act of folly. Here is my virgin daughter and his concubine. Please let me bring them out that you may ravish them and do to them whatever you wish. But do not commit such an act of folly against this man.'"** (Pause: Holy shit, are you kidding me? Tell me this is not real!)

"But the men would not listen to him. So the Levite seized his concubine and brought her out to them; and they raped her and abused her all night until morning, then let her go at the approach of dawn. As the day began to dawn, the woman came and fell down at the doorway of the old man's house where her master was, until full daylight."

The thought of all of these men being so insensitive to the feelings and safety of another human being is sick. Such is the value of women in the Bible. To be so indifferent to the female sex and the responsibility of marriage, and so unconcerned about her welfare, that he would sacrifice his wife to save his own skin. Was he punishing her for being unfaithful to him? So much for forgiveness. If so, the punishment was far greater than the sin. How was this Levite able to lie down and go to sleep while the townsmen were abusing his wife in the street! How calloused can a man become? Well, hang on to your seats. It does get even worse.

Let us return to this awful account. **"When her master arose in the morning and opened the doors of the house and went out to go on his way, then behold, his concubine** [aka wife] **was lying at the doorway of the house with her hands on the threshold. He said to her, 'Get up and let us go,' but there was no answer. Then he placed her on the donkey; and the man arose and went to his home. When he entered his house, he took a knife and laid hold of his concubine** [aka wife] **and cut her in twelve pieces, limb by limb, and sent her throughout the territory of Israel. All who saw it said, 'Nothing like this has ever happened or been seen from the day when the sons of Israel came up from the land of Egypt to this day. Consider it, take counsel and speak up!'"**

What a despicable account! The Levite desecrates and mutilates his wife's corpse by cutting it into twelve parts and FedExing one part to each of the twelve tribes of Israel. Of course, he wants to mobilize the support of the tribes and punish the men of Gibeah who have killed his wife, but in fact, he was the one who had let them kill her! Surely there were other ways to call attention to Gibeah's crime.

Had the Levite gone to Shiloh where the tabernacle stood (18:31), and had he consulted with the high priest, he could have dealt with the matter and avoided causing a great deal of trouble. Once tempers were heated in Israel, however, it was difficult to stop the fire from spreading. The outrage escalates into a full-scale civil war that almost destroys the tribe of Benjamin.

In chapter 20, the war begins. The tribes of Israel gather together in unison and prepare to pour out their wrath on their own brethren, now the perverts of Gibeah. They take three vows: (1) no one will go home until Gibeah is attacked and destroyed; (2) anyone who does not join against Gibeah will be killed; and (3) no one will allow his daughter to marry a Benjamite.

Ironically, Israel is finally unified as "one nation." However, they are unified in their quest for vengeance against their own. Unfortunately, the Levite testifies against the men of Gibeah without owning his sin. Naturally, not knowing the full story, the Israelites are all the more infuriated. When the Israelites approach the Benjamites, they refuse to hand over the men who committed the atrocity. Instead, they decide to go to war with Israel. So twenty-six thousand plus Benjamites go to war with over four hundred thousand Israelites! Is this civil war God's will? The men of Gibeah are evil men and have to be punished. In order to please the Lord and cleanse his people, the sinners must be cleansed from his land. Don't forget, these are all God's people and the Lord has been continually busy cleansing his land of all the sinners ever since the time of Noah.

When sin isn't exposed, confessed, and punished, it pollutes society and defiles the land. The wicked men of Gibeah are like a cancerous tumour in the body that has to be cut out.

When God's people refuse to obey God's Word, the results are always tragic. It is interesting that the all-knowing God shuts his eyes to the sins of the Levite and will not discipline him. God holds the opinion that there can never be unity among his people as long as some of them cover up sin and allow it to infect the body. There you have it: God is a hypocrite. (**Pause:** Before you get carried away, don't forget these are all stories written by men — illiterate, superstitious, imbecilic men.)

Back to this man-made story. So under the Lord's instruction, Judah leads the charge against the twenty-six thousand Benjamite warriors. The Benjamites manage to kill twenty-two thousand Israelites the first day of battle. The Israelites weep before the Lord because of their loss and question whether they should continue their attack. Perhaps this was one reason why God permitted the Israelites to lose that first battle. It gave them an opportunity to reflect on the fact that they were fighting their own flesh and blood. The Lord instructs them to attack, but the Benjamites kill eighteen thousand Israelites that day. The whole Israelite army go up to Bethel, where they fast and weep before the Lord. They offer sacrifices to the Lord and inquire once again if they should continue to attack.

(**Pause:** Let's go back a bit. I thought there were twenty-six thousand Benjamites and four hundred thousand Israelites? On the first two days of battle, a total of forty thousand Israelites were killed. How many Benjamites were killed? The book of Judges doesn't say. And I thought these Israelites were great warriors. They sure are in need of a king.)

Let us continue. The Lord instructs the Israelites (God loves a good fight) to attack once again, but this time he assures them of victory (20:28).

The Israelites set an ambush and then feigned defeat, so that the Benjamites pressed their attack, leaving the safety of the city. The retreating forces then turned around and went on the attack. The battle was fierce, but when the day was over 25,100 Benjamite warriors had been slain in battle. The Benjamite army was decimated. Only 600 soldiers survived and fled to the rock of Rimmon (20:47). The Israelites then completely destroyed the Benjamite cities, just as they had annihilated the Canaanites (20:48). Such is the price the tribe of Benjamin paid for pissing off God!

In chapter 21, it appears that Israel develops a hint of a conscience. They weep over the fact that the tribe of Benjamin will be eliminated from Israel. So instead of consulting the Lord, they develop a scheme to preserve Benjamin. But instead of getting directions from the Lord, the eleven tribes depend on their own wisdom to solve the problem. The six hundred men who were left from Benjamin would need wives if they were going to re-establish their tribe, but the eleven tribes had sworn not to give them wives. Where would these wives come from? The Israelites solved the problem by killing more of their own people! Nobody had come to the war from Jabesh-Gilead, which meant two things: They hadn't participated in the oath, and the city deserved to be punished. The executioners found four hundred virgins in the city, women who could become wives to two-thirds of the soldiers on the rock. These men had been on the rock for four months (20:47), but now they could take their brides and go home. What price was paid for these wives?

The elders held another meeting to discuss how they could provide wives for the remaining two hundred men. Somebody remembered that many of the virgins from the tribes participated in an annual feast at Shiloh.

If the remaining two hundred men of Benjamin hid near the place, they could each kidnap a girl and take her home as a wife. The tribes wouldn't be violating their oath because they wouldn't be *giving* the girls as brides. The girls were being *taken*. It was a matter of semantics, but they agreed to follow the plan. Thus, the six hundred men got their brides, the eleven tribes kept their vow, the citizens of Gibeah were punished, the tribe of Benjamin was taught a lesson, and the twelve tribes of Israel were saved.

The six hundred men of Benjamin, with their brides, returned to their inheritance, cleaned up the debris, repaired the cities, and started life all over again (21:19–24). In some ways, it is a fitting end to this record of such a tragic period in Israel's history. In the end, the Israelites are no better than the Canaanites whom they were to dispossess.

So there you have it. If you need a wife, just help yourself and kidnap a virgin. She must, however, be a virgin.

Isn't that nice!

~

The Slaughter of the Midianites

"If the bible be true, God commanded his chosen people to destroy men simply for the crime of defending their native land. They were not allowed to spare trembling and white-haired age, nor dimpled babes clasped in the mothers' arms. They were ordered to kill women, and to pierce, with the sword of war, the unborn child. 'Our heavenly Father' commanded the Hebrews to kill the men and women, the fathers, sons and brothers, but to preserve the girls alive. Why were not the maidens also killed? Why were they spared? Read the thirty-first chapter of Numbers, and you will find that the maidens were given to the soldiers and the priests. Is there, in all the history of war, a more infamous thing than this? Is it possible that God permitted the violets of modesty, that grow and shed their perfume in the maiden's heart, to be trampled beneath the brutal feet of lust? If this was the order of God, what, under the same circumstances, would have been the command of a devil? When, in this age of the world, a woman, a wife, a mother, reads this record, she should, with scorn and loathing, throw the book away. A general, who now should make such an order, giving over to massacre and rapine a conquered people, would be held in execration by the whole civilized world. Yet, if the bible be true, the supreme and infinite God was once a savage."

—Robert G. Ingersoll

The Slaughter of the Midianites

"He killed all those people every male. They had offended the Deity in some way. We know what the offence was, without looking; that is to say, we know it was a trifle; some small thing that no one but a god would attach any importance to. It is more than likely that a Midianite had been duplicating the conduct of one Onan, who was commanded to 'go into his brother's wife' — which he did; but instead of finishing, 'he spilled it on the ground.' The Lord slew Onan for that, for the Lord could never abide indelicacy.

"Some Midianite must have repeated Onan's act, and brought that dire disaster upon his nation. If that was not the indelicacy that outraged the feelings of the Deity, then I know what it was: some Midianite had been pissing against the wall. I am sure of it, for that was an impropriety which the Source of all Etiquette never could stand. A person could piss against a tree, he could piss on his mother, he could piss on his own breeches, and get off, but he must not piss against the wall, that would be going quite too far.

"The origin of the divine prejudice against this humble crime is not stated; but we know that the prejudice was very strong so strong that nothing but a wholesale massacre of the people inhabiting the region where the wall was defiled could satisfy the Deity."

—Mark Twain: Satan, writing back to his friends in heaven upon visiting Earth, this time discussing the biblical tale of "The Slaughter of the Midianites" in Numbers 31, in *Letters from the Earth* (1909?; published in 1962).

All during this time, the Israelites, and all their various tribes and leaders, were fighting, killing, raping, lying and stealing among each other. It seemed as though it did not matter — all the miracles performed by Moses and the messages delivered from God were ignored. Boy, are these people stupid or what? The parting of the Red Sea alone would have convinced me. Be it as it may, there was a whole lot more killing to be done, as the writers of the Bible seem to delight in telling these tales.

Before we get into the slaughtering of the Midianites (Numbers 31), there is another little story that only an idiot would believe, let alone write about. I cannot leave these dumbass Bible stories without telling you about the talking donkey. That's right, first we have the talking snake, but he was Satan, so that helped to make the unbelievable a bit more believable. The story of the talking donkey is in Numbers 22:22–34.

So this chap Balaam, apparently an Amorite — another of the Israelites tribes gone bad — was sent by a King Balak on some kind of journey. He is riding his donkey when the donkey sees an invisible angel with a sword. The angel was apparently sent by God to obstruct Balaam. (Do you believe this?) Why didn't God just send a lightning bolt to eliminate Mr. B.? Well, only the donkey sees the invisible angel and tries to go around him. Balaam gets upset with the donkey's manoeuvre and beats him.

The same thing happens again. The donkey is afraid of God's invisible angel, as he thinks the angel is about to drive the sword through him. The next time the donkey sees the angel, he just sits down and won't move and Balaam beats the donkey again.

Now we go from the ridiculous (with a donkey seeing an invisible angel with a sword) to a donkey (with some divine help) being able to talk. So the donkey says, *"Hey, what the hell is the matter with you? Stop beating me, you idiot. Haven't I been a good ass and served you faithfully?"*

Now Balaam, not the least bit surprised that his donkey is suddenly able to talk, shoots back, *"If I had my sword, I'd kill you right on the spot."*

At this point, the Lord intervenes, and the angel carrying a sword sets Balaam straight, admonishes him for the way he treated his donkey, when his loyal beast was only trying his best to avoid a problem for Balaam. As the angel continues to explain, Balaam apologizes to the angel and he receives his new marching orders from the angel. Life just goes on as if a talking donkey is an everyday occurrence. And people actually believe this stuff.

Enough of talking donkeys. Let's get on with some more of God's killings. As it came to pass, the Lord said to Moses, *"Hey Mo, wake up! It's time to do some more avenging."*

Numbers 31:1–3 *"And the LORD spake unto Moses, saying, Avenge the children of Israel of the Midianites: afterward shalt thou be gathered unto thy people. And Moses spake unto the people, saying, Arm some of yourselves unto the war, and let them go against the Midianites."*

The Bible doesn't say how many fighting men Moses was able to assemble, but it was easily into the many thousands. In reality, call it what you want, but God ordered genocide. He commanded the Israelites to slaughter all Midianite males (including infants) and all adult Midianite women who had lain with a man.

He commanded that the young girls who supposedly had not lain with a man be tested for virginity and given to their captors as sex slaves. What exactly is the recommended testing procedure for virgins?

Numbers 31:15-18 (I'll paraphrase.) After killing all the men, Moses ordered his army officers to kill all of the male children and all of the non-virgin females, but to save all the virgin girls for his troops. The invading Israelites took all of the animals and goods of the Midianites and then burned all of their towns. Genocide may be a war crime today, but back then when Moses followed the word of God, it is known as *"Divine Command Theory"* and is morally acceptable. I learned this theory from Professor William Lane Craig.

So Moses, who had some years earlier delivered God's word — *"Thou shalt not kill"* — had no problem ordering this horrendous act of genocide.

The great Mo, of course, justified it as his pal Yahweh, the God of Israel, ordered him to do this, because the Midianites worshiped a deity named Baal Peor. The Midianites forgot the First Commandment. For the act of worshiping a false god, the so-called real god wiped them out. If this real god ever returns, he will have to wipe out a few billion more people who have their own false god.

I may be mistaken here, but it seems God's actions are a tad inconsistent with goodness, kindness and love. But then, perhaps I misunderstand the crimes of murder, rape, enslavement and child abuse.

Following all the rape and pillage, the captives are brought before Moses, who condemns to death all the male children and all the non-virginal women.

Numbers 31:17 *"Now therefore kill every male among the little ones, and kill every woman that hath known man by lying with him."*

Talk about a bloodthirsty bastard! Now I ask, how many of you have heard this story on Sunday in church? Everyone raise your hand. You would be hard-pressed to see a single hand raised.

Moses then encourages his men to use the female children for (presumably) sexual pleasure. You may think I am kidding. Read for yourself.

Numbers 31:18 *"But all the women children, that have not known a man by lying with him, keep alive for yourselves."*

I am being repetitive, but some things suffer repeating.

- God orders genocide in a most cruel, painful and suffering manner.
- God, by demanding such carnage, is clearly a monster.
- Not a single man is spared. (Does anyone really think they were all bad people?)
- All the Midianite boys and non-virginal women are ordered to their deaths.
- The Israelite men are encouraged to enslave and rape the virgin Midianite girls.

By any measurement, most civilized people would condemn such actions as these. They would be considered so evil that a commission on crimes against humanity would seek justice upon the architect of such horrors. Instead of condemnation and denunciation, millions of religious people praise this monster they call God.

King David – The Killing Machine

David and Goliath,
by Osmar Schindler (c. 1888)

David hoists the severed head of Goliath
as illustrated by Gustave Doré (1866).

King David – The Killing Machine

Who was King David?

We know the Bible is full of contradictions. We know (although some resist the charge) that the Bible is just another fairy tale. The story of David fills this description of both contradictions and fairy tale. Yet, you will find vigorous defenders of King David, especially those of the Jewish faith.

As I've said many times throughout this book, I am no authority on the Bible. I am certainly no authority on the supposed life of David. King David of Israel plays a big role in the Old Testament. It would be ludicrous to attempt to do justice to all his exploits. This would take an entire book by itself.

To get another view of King David, I recommend Steve Wells's book *Drunk with Blood*. Steve Wells devotes a good portion of his book to the killings of David in pages 144–176. His stinging, irreverent and humorous commentary is enlightening.

My reading of David is incomplete. This is an abridged version, and it is viewed through a prism of skepticism and ignorance. It is truly a layman's take on the life of David.

Before I really got into reading the Bible, all I knew of "David" was the following, and I did not know much of these:
- David kills Goliath
- The Star of David
- The City of David
- The House of David

What do these four points mean? First, let us take the killing of Goliath. This was a beautiful little story, much like "Jack and the Beanstalk," wherein Jack triumphs over the giant. Here we have a nice little shepherd boy who slays the giant Goliath and saves his people from being slaughtered. This is what I was told in Sunday school over sixty years ago. That is how the story ended. What they failed to tell me, either in Sunday school or later in church, was that David proceeded to cut off the head of Goliath. Nice!

Can you believe that this naïve former Christian did not know of David's gruesome act, and many other hideous ones, until a few years ago? Talk about someone who had his head in the sand, or perhaps in another place where the sun doesn't shine — that was me!

I even knew less about the Star of David. It was just an unfamiliar term to me. You will not find a consensus on this one, just like many other issues. Some say it is an occult symbol, others say its represents the Morning Star, others say it was on the Shield of David, others on the Ring of Solomon, others say it represents sexuality, unity, fire and water and a host of other things. Take your pick!

In any event, at some point in history the Jewish people, or their religion, adopted it as a universal symbol of the State of Israel, even if a reliable history can not be confirmed.

The City of David is no less confusing than the Star of David. Like much else in the Bible, you will find references to the City of David being one in its own or holding the name of Zion, Jerusalem or Bethlehem. I'll let the scholars debate this one, as you can see the writers of various books of the Bible have a difficult time singing from the same song sheet.

Now we come to the House of David. I am not going to even try to unravel this convoluted genealogy, which is composed of some of the most hideous, revolting, shocking, repulsive and repugnant characters in the entire Bible. And yet, the biblical King David is revered by Jews to this day.

From the following website: http://unitedwithisrael.org/act-now-keep-tomb-of-king-david-under-israeli-control/ — A popular song, in fact, the first song that many Jewish children learn, contains only the words: *"David Melech Israel Hai Vekayam"* — Hebrew for *"David King of Israel lives forever"* — referring to his legacy that will never be forgotten by Jews of faith.

Let us take a closer look at this the great King of Israel.

He is depicted as a righteous king, although not without faults, as well as an acclaimed warrior, musician and poet, traditionally credited for composing many of the psalms contained in the Book of Psalms.

David is an important figure to members of the Jewish, Christian and Islamic faiths. Biblical tradition maintains the Messiah's direct descent from the line of David. In Islam, he is considered a prophet. For God, David seems able to do no wrong and is regularly forgiven for his sins. He remains one of God's most favoured of all his killers.

Space will not permit me to address all of the fights, battles, skirmishes, confrontations or killings that David either committed himself or played a part in. Suffice it to say this fellow was extremely busy in the area of killing, as well as some other questionable behaviour in this dysfunctional House of David.

It would be impossible to summarize King David's exploits. But I will give it my best shot. David claims to have killed a lion and a bear with his bare hands. (And I used to think Davey Crockett was something.) He then kills a giant with a slingshot (and don't forget the part about slicing off Goliath's head), then it comes time to do some more killing and Saul and David go about, apparently separately, to kill some Philistines.

Saul, the current King of Israel, is quite happy with killing a few thousand Philistines in battle, but little David kills Philistines in the tens of thousands.

It is at this point that things get a bit goofy. The young ladies of Israel are taken with the young, handsome David and proceed to dance, sing and celebrate David's massive killings. Young David becomes their hero once again. King Saul sees David as a threat and enemy and tries to kill David. This doesn't work out too well, so I guess old Saul lives by the edict *"Keep your friends close, but keep your enemies closer."*

Saul tries to convince David to marry one of his daughters. David feels he, a mere shepherd, is not worthy of marrying a king's daughter, and besides, he has nothing to offer. The still-scheming king figures another battle with the Philistines might just finish this little bastard off once and for all.

He makes a deal with David. Saul promotes David as commander over his armies and offers him his daughter Michal in marriage if he will bring back one hundred foreskins of the Philistines (kinky?). The proud David is feeling up to the challenge, as such a victory would serve the king's wishes and make him worthy to be his son-in-law; David agrees.

This little imp David, instead of doing the right thing and getting himself killed, takes his men and kills not one hundred but two hundred Philistines. He then proceeds to cut their little dicks and bring back their foreskins. The optics of this mass circumcision is too much to picture, even for a fairy tale. Can you imagine a pastor telling this story in church? Hey — it's right there in the Bible!

They count out the full number of foreskins to the king. This must have been another interesting sight to behold. Imagine David's men in front of King Saul, counting one foreskin, two foreskins, three foreskins, all the way until they reach two hundred foreskins?

Saul then gives David his daughter Michal in marriage.

David continues his killings and is successful in many battles. The more his popularity grows among the people, the more Saul wants this hero of the people killed. Saul tries to arrange for David's death, but his plots fail. A number of other curious events take place, and a lot more killings, before David becomes King David.

This king that Jews revere is far from a nice fellow. He is indeed a warrior, of that there is no doubt. After yet another slaughter, of the Ammonites, this is what David does with the survivors...according to the King James Version of II Samuel 12:31.

"And he brought forth the people that were therein, and put them under saws, and under harrows of iron, and under the axes of iron, and made them pass through the brickkiln: and thus did he unto all the cities of the children of Ammon. So David and all the people returned unto Jerusalem."

Are these atrocities any different than the cruel acts from the Holocaust of World War II? If we condemn the Nazis for their atrocities, why should we not do the same for David's bloodthirsty actions? But wait!

Here is the New International Version interpretation of II Samuel 12: 29–31. Verses 29–30 are close to the same in both versions of the Bible, as it goes like this:

29–30 (NIV*) "So David mustered the entire army and went to Rabbah, and attacked and captured it. David took the crown from their king's head, and it was placed on his own head. It weighed a talent of gold, and it was set with precious stones. David took a great quantity of plunder from the city."*

Now take a look at how Verse 31 of the NIV of the Bible differs from the KJV. *"And he brought out the people who were there, consigning them to labour with saws and with iron picks and axes, and he made them work at brick making. David did this to all the Ammonite towns. Then he and his entire army returned to Jerusalem."*

Take your pick as to which version you want to believe.

King Saul met his death at the hands of the Philistines. I Samuel 31: 6–10 KJV. It is recorded it this way:

"So Saul died, and his three sons, and his armourbearer, and all his men, that same day together. And when the men of Israel that were *on the other side of the valley, and* they *that* were *on the other side Jordan, saw that the men of Israel fled, and that Saul and his sons were dead, they forsook the cities, and fled; and the Philistines came and dwelt in them....*

"And it came to pass on the morrow, when the Philistines came to strip the slain, that they found Saul and his three sons fallen in mount Gilboa. And they cut off his head, and stripped off his armour, and sent into the land of the Philistines round about, to publish it in the house of their idols, and among the people. And they put his armour in the house of Ashtaroth: and they fastened his body to the wall of Bethshan."

After a few thousand years, one would think this barbaric act of beheading people would have been discarded by civilized people. When it comes to religious fanatics, not much has changed. I'll digress from the story of David to show present-day killing rituals.

By Dan Bloom - Published: | Updated: 22:04 GMT, 27 July 2014

"Islamist militants have reportedly beheaded dozens of soldiers at a Syrian army base and mounted their heads on poles. Extremists from the group Islamic State, previously known as ISIS, seized the base in the northern province of Raqqa, leaving more than 85 soldiers dead and 200 more unaccounted for. The Syrian Human Rights Observatory said at least 50 of the soldiers had been executed — many of them beheaded — as horrifying footage began circulating online which appeared to show the bodies.'

Read more: http://www.dailymail.co.uk/news/article-2707322/Heads-sticks-Sick-ISIS-video-emerges-showing-50-beheaded-Syrian-soldiers-impaled-poles-held-aloft-Raqqa-city.html#ixzz3MIxkVdt8

David, and later, as King David, continues to enjoy one enormously long stretch of killings. All of this killing being done with either the approval of the invisible muppet in the sky…or by the Almighty's decree. Throughout, David runs afoul with his god, argues with his god, and at times gets a bit chippy; but God regularly forgives David his sins and immediately dispatches David to do some more killing. Needless to say, God's partnership with David seems to work out well for both of them.

There is one more interesting story about the strange behaviour of this so-called "righteous" king.

Uriah was a soldier in King David's army. He was the husband of Bathsheba. One day, David the voyeur watches as Bathsheba is taking a bath, in the nude, of course. David's testosterone kicks in, and the righteous monarch seduces the lady. How could Mrs. B. refuse a king? David lays big red in between the loins of the irresistible wife of his loyal soldier. As fate would have it, Bathsheba gets pregnant. Of course, it is her fault.

All of this causes a bit of problem for the good king. David orders the return of Uriah from the front lines and tells his loyal friend to take a break from his fighting and to go lie with his wife. "Lie" is the Bible's way of saying *"get it on"* with your wife. Now this causes some confusion in Uriah's mind, as it was custom to not have sex while in active duty. Apparently sex drains one of one's strength.

Uriah thinks this is a test of his loyalty, and he refuses to have sex with Bathsheba. Now David is really getting frustrated. A little nooky between the couple could have hidden the adulterous nature of her pregnancy by David. David now needs to take drastic action.

He sends Uriah back into battle with a private message that Uriah is to give to the general of David's army. The private message instructs the general to put Uriah in the front of the lines of the battle, where it is the most dangerous. In effect, David delivers Uriah into the hands of the enemy. David has Uriah carry the private message that orders his own death. Shakespeare himself could not have written a more devious scheme.

After Uriah is dead, David makes the now-widowed Bathsheba his wife and all is well. There you go, everything all taken care of nice and tidy-like. But wait! There is more to this story. David's troubles are not over yet.

Here is what the Bible says: 2 Samuel 11:27 (KJV)

*"And when the mourning was past, David sent and fetched her to his house, and she became his wife, and bare him a son. **But the thing that David had done displeased the LORD.**"*

Isn't this interesting? The big guy in the sky was watching this entire episode take place and did nothing. However, this bloodlust god had a plan. He always has a plan.

The next verse in the Bible starts a new chapter. II Samuel – Chapter 12:1 reads as follows:

"And the LORD sent Nathan unto David. And he came unto him, and said unto him, There were two men in one city; the one rich, and the other poor."

Nathan is a prophet. He proceeds to tell David a story and gives David a tongue-lashing. I won't go into all of this.

David, after being thoroughly told by Nathan what a naughty boy he is, now confesses his multiple sins of adultery, killing Uriah and so forth. So much for the Ten Commandments.

Needless to say, it is time for God to implement his plan and punish David. What does this loving god do? A few days after Bathsheba gives birth to David's child, the baby dies. Nice plan, eh? God just loves to kill innocent little babies. It wasn't the baby's fault that he was born of an adulterous relationship. Why kill the baby?

This totally stupid god continues to act as some kind of imbecilic human being (just like whoever wrote the Bible's story of David), and all is forgiven. David then proceeds to have another child named Solomon, who becomes the next king. This Solomon chap with his harem of one thousand is no better than his father, David. And yet all I ever heard about Solomon when I went to Sunday school was how wise this rotten bastard was.

If anyone who is religious can square this circle, then you are truly delusional.

As John Donne said, don't bother trying.

"Go not thou about to square either circle (God or thyself)." — John Donne, 1624

I received some help from the following, but for the most part the above is my take on *"David the Killing Machine."*

http://en.wikipedia.org/wiki/David

http://www.nobeliefs.com/DarkBible/darkbible3.htm

https://www.biblegateway.com/passage/?search=1+Chronicles+18&version=NIRV

https://answers.yahoo.com/question/index?qid=20120413135250AA2AwDR

http://dictionary.reference.com/browse/square+the+circle

~

Religion and the Church Today

"Gott Mit Uns" means "God with Us"

(on Nazi soldiers belt buckles during WWII.)

"I believe that I am acting in accordance with the will of the Almighty Creator: by defending myself against the Jew, I am fighting for the work of the Lord."

— Adolph Hitler
(Both God and Hitler loved to kill, especially Jews)

The Philosophy of Life

"It's obnoxious to abbreviate the human capacity to inflict pain, remorse and suffering...all in the pretence of humanity."

—My Father, (Bernard James Hinkley)

The Philosophy of Life

(With a little help from the philosopher Voltaire)

George was a thoughtful, kind and considerate young man. He hadn't set his course in life yet. He came from a good family. His parents were middle class. His father was an insurance broker, and his mother an elementary school teacher.

George recently graduated from university with a business degree but wasn't sure what he wanted to do. He questioned many things about society. His family was moderately religious. They would discuss politics, the economy and current affairs, but were not activists in any sense. George was confused about many things. He could never understand the injustice in the world. Why did so many children suffer from diseases, die young or go to bed hungry? Why were there so many wars? He was conflicted about religious dogma. He was disturbed over the huge disparity between the wealthy and the poor in society.

All of these things he would think about and question. He wondered why the world was the way it was. Could it ever be changed? Could society become more caring, more sharing, less violent? His uncle Charlie, his father's brother, was quite close to George. Charlie was a practical man. He didn't suffer fools. He called it the way he saw it. Some folks had difficulty with his direct, no-nonsense way of dealing with life. You would never see Charlie crying in his beer. Self-pity was not part of Charlie's character. Yet he was always there to give a helping hand or a word of advice — even if you didn't ask.

Charlie was an atheist, but didn't broadcast it. He was disgusted with organized religion.

One day George asked his uncle Charlie why there was so much injustice, unfairness and evil in society. Uncle Charlie had been there before. Many years ago, Charlie had experienced the same personal dilemma as George. One could chalk it up to the blind idealism of youth or the lack of worldly experience. Over time Charlie was able to reconcile all of the questions that George was struggling with. This only happened after he gave up religion. Yes, at one time Charlie was a believer; that was until he started reading the Bible.

Uncle Charlie said something to George that stuck with him for the rest of his life. He said, *"Do no harm, expect nothing, and be responsible for your own actions. If you follow this creed, don't worry about the rest."* George remembers Charlie saying, *"The rich, the powerful and the evil have always been with us and probably always will."*

Uncle Charlie told his nephew a story about another young man who questioned many of the same things that bothered George. His name was Angelo. One night Angelo had a dream. At least he thought it was a dream. And yet it seemed so very real to Angelo.

On that unforgettable night, a genie, a ghost or some kind of spirit appeared to him. The spirit transported Angelo into a desert. The desert was piled up with large heaps of old bones. The stench of rotted flesh filled the air, and Angelo gagged. It was all he could do to hold back from vomiting on the spot. The bones of the dead formed a wall on each side of long pathways as far as the eye could see. The piles were so high that you could not see over them.

The bones were in rows upon rows, and at the end of each row were walks of tall evergreens. The evergreens were the most beautiful, tall, stately trees that nature has ever produced. All were perfect in size and form. At the end of the walks stood three men covered in long white robes. They stood in a plush garden. Their faces were ashen and without expression. Flowers of every colour and fragrance were surrounded by hedges flawlessly trimmed to perfection. Songbirds fluttered about. It was picture perfect. A regular Garden of Eden.

Angelo was confused. He asked the Spirit, *"Why did you bring me to see such horrible things and then such a beautiful garden? Who are these patriarchs that stand motionless?"* The Spirit replied, *"You shall know, poor human creature, but first you must cry, and then through your tears you will learn and finally you will accept."*

The spirit took Angelo through more rows of bones. *"These bones here,"* said the Spirit, *"are the twenty thousand Jews who danced before a calf, with the twenty-four thousand who were killed while lying with Midianitish women."* The sum of all those massacred for such offences amounts to nearly three hundred thousand.

In another row were the bones of Christians slaughtered by others over four centuries of disputes. One heap was so high it mounted into the sky and needed to be divided several times. In another row were piled the bones of Muslims who were sullied by the same inhumanities, but pity was not a tribute to their sacrifice. As for all the other nations, each had their own pile of bones, and rotting flesh, because of their religious wars, superstitious beliefs, greed and lust for power.

Angelo shouted, *"My God! Why did you leave these frightful bones to rot in the desert sun? The stink is a dishonour to the souls of all these poor men, women and children. Should they not be buried and out of sight?"* The Spirit slowly looked upon Angelo and said, *"Should they?"*

Angelo protested, *"But this is an abomination. These are monuments to barbarism and fanaticism."* *"So,"* said the Spirit, *"you begin to understand."* Angelo could not suppress his emotions any longer. He cried, and his tears flowed like the rivers of the earth. *"But why do you weep?"* asked the Spirit. *"Is this not the truth? Weeping is of no use. So now you must learn,"* said the Spirit. *"Learn what?"* asked Angelo. The Spirit said, *"Learn that which has caused you such pain, that you may deal with the pain and understand life."*

Angelo pleaded with the Spirit. *"I don't want to see any more bones."* The Spirit said, *"But we have barely begun. I have so much more to show you. I have millions of more bones in rows and rows. You have much to learn."* Angelo cried, *"Please, please, no more, I beg of you."* The Spirit said, *"Then let us move to another place."* Angelo heaved a sigh of relief.

It was then that Angelo saw a man of gentle, simple countenance, who seemed to be about thirty-five years of age. From afar Angelo noticed his feet were swollen and bleeding, his hands too, his side pierced, and his ribs flayed with whip cuts. *"Good Heavens. Why was this man treated in such a hateful way?"* The Spirit said, *"Wicked priests and judges conspired to poison all that he professed. He was guilty of challenging their authority."* *"He must have done more to receive such horrible treatment,"* cried Angelo.

"O, yes he did," said the Spirit. *"There is a legend that claims he would heal the sick, comfort the lonely, and feed the poor and hungry." "So he was a religious man?"* queried Angelo. *"No,"* said the Spirit, *"he had no religion. He had a simple creed: 'Love your fellow creatures as yourself.'"*

Angelo exclaimed, *"This makes no sense!" "Well there is more; you see, the mythology of this man grew and grew,"* said the Spirit. *"As the years passed, many different scribes made up stories. The stories grew and changed until this man was deemed the son of God. The myth grew, and a religion developed in his name. Over the centuries, millions of people were slain as other religions claimed their religion was the one true religion. The competing religions resulted in years of bloodshed."* The Spirit stopped talking and all went quiet as Angelo, in a state of shock, stood motionless as he pondered all what the Spirit had said.

Then the Spirit was about to disappear. *"Wait!"* yelled Angelo. *"Yes,"* said the Spirit. *"You are talking about Jesus,"* cried Angelo. *"Jesus? No, I am not talking about the myth of Jesus...I am talking about the reality of religion. The one so-called Jesus is a myth, but religion is a reality,"* said the Spirit.

"But why do you leave these millions upon millions of human bones?" asked Angelo. *"It is a reminder of what religion, greed and oppression does to mankind,"* said the Spirit. *"But who are the three patriarchs we saw earlier?"* Angelo asked. The Spirit said, *"One represents all the religions of the world, the other all the wealthy of the world and the other all the powerful of the world."*

The Spirit continued, *"They live in the lap of luxury, a lush garden that serves their every need, but it brings them no happiness. Their sullen faces show they have lost their humanity. Even though they control the minds of the people with religious doctrine; even though they control the people with crumbs of bread; even though they control the people through physical violence and government oppression; they are infected by greed, power and the obsession to control."*

The Spirit disappeared, and Angelo woke up.

Charlie ended his story and didn't say a word more. He waited and watched George's face. A few moments of silence seemed like an eternity. It was like a wall had been erected between the older man and the young man. George lifted up his head and looked squarely into the eyes of his uncle. Finally, George broke the silence.

"Uncle Charlie, are you saying that religion, the wealthy and the powerful are the cause of poverty, wars and misery?" asked George.

Uncle Charlie, in a slow deliberate manner, asked George to think back over all of history. He asked George to think about the overwhelming number of wars and acts of inhumanity and asked, *"What was the root cause of these conflicts?"*

"The evidence will show that religious dogma, greed and lust for control are dominant reasons for most of the killings and suffering in the world," Uncle Charlie said in disgust.

"George," Charlie said, *"let me tell you something. The day is now here; we live in a world where religion, government and the wealthy currently rule the entire world. When all three eventually consolidate so that neither is distinguishable from the other, that is the day when the world, as we know it, will come to an end."*

When George spoke, he looked like a different person. In a quiet tone, he said, *"Thank you, Uncle Charlie. I think I now understand."*

~

A Religious Man

"I mean, you could claim that **anything's** *real if the only basis for believing in it is that nobody's* proved *it doesn't exist!"*

— J.K. Rowling

"If you win a person's heart you may also control his mind; but if you control his mind, you don't necessarily win his heart."

— Brian Hinkley

A Religious Man

John was an ordinary man. He was good, he was honest, and he was a practical man. He was a family man. He believed when you give a good day's work, you deserve a fair wage. He had an old-fashioned work ethic that many would scoff at today. John held to a sense of fairness and thought that greed was the worst of the seven deadly sins. He did not believe in fancy things. Indulgences, he had few. He came from a family that had no luxuries. Every penny was spent or saved wisely. His mother and father never owned a new car or ever bought a new house. All of his clothes were hand-me-downs from his older brothers.

Manual labour was not something to be ashamed of; not in the least. As a young boy he looked forward to the day when one of his older brothers outgrew their clothes. He waited patiently for years to inherit an old jean jacket. Though it was frayed around the edges and one of the buttonholes was now too big to hold tight the button, John was excited beyond words when he finally claimed this prized old jacket from his big brother. He wore that jacket with pride as he strutted around the neighbourhood like a proud peacock. That's how it was. John grew up with values conceived in another era. His humble approach, at one time, was commonplace. Today it seems archaic and naïve.

John wanted to go to college, but that was unheard of when John was a boy. Grade school and a bit of high school education was all that could be expected. At fifteen years of age, it was work. Work of any kind. John soon learned to use his wits and his hands. Most of what he learned was passed on to him from family, friends and neighbours. Part-time work would help hone his skills. He liked to take things apart to see how they worked.

He soon learned how things were made and how to repair or replace broken parts. He was curious and possessed a questioning mind.

John regretted not completing high school or going to college. He liked to read. He would read almost anything, from the back of milk cartons, cereal boxes, comic books and, yes, the classics. He was initiated into the classics through the comics. He was lucky enough to have an elderly neighbour who had a stack of what looked like comic books. These were books about Tom Sawyer and Huck Finn, works of Charles Dickens and, yes, even Shakespeare. But they were in comic book form, with brightly coloured pictures that encouraged children to read. In later life, this grounding in the classics provided him the encouragement to read other classics.

There is a strange irony with John. He was a religious man. However, he never actually read the Bible. When it came to religion, John did not question its teachings. In his youth he went to Sunday school, and later, church. Like many children he just accepted all that was preached from the pulpit without question. John is a paradox because in all else he was full of curiosity and constantly questioned everything. He passed on this practice of blind faith to his own children. He and his family dutifully attended church and did what he thought the Almighty wanted him to do.

When his children would ask questions like, *"Did Jesus actually walk on water?"* or *"Did Jesus actually bring a dead man back to life?'* John would simply say, *"If that's what it says in the Bible then it must be true."*

And yet, with everything else, John dealt with life in a practical, thoughtful, reasoned manner.

His inquisitive mind sparked a burning desire to know everything about how machines operated, how plants grew, and why the stars glowed. Then, without missing a beat, he would have reservations about the sanity of those who believed in fairies and leprechauns. But when it came to religion, spirits and an invisible god, all seemed real, as it was his unquestioning faith that guided his thinking.

John is a commonsensical man, who had read some of the great literary works, except he shunned any critical writings of the Bible. Through the years he never read the Bible, except for a few passages. One is left to ponder how a commonsensical thinking man can be dominated by religious dogma. One is left to ask, what is stronger, the logical thoughts of the mind or the emotional passions in the depths of a man's heart? It would appear that if you win a person's heart, you also control his mind; but if you control his mind, you don't necessarily win his heart.

Good sense and plain reason, which explains the natural world, gives way to ignorance when one believes the incredible claims of the supernatural and superstition. People like John, who believe in the religious supernatural, are not stupid. They lack wit. This does not mean they lack humour. Rather, their otherwise normal ability to perceive and understand is being blocked by a controlling force. That controlling force is faith and religion. The force is so powerful that it has the uncanny ability to both win hearts and control minds. Folks like John are not consciously aware of this controlling force. They just accept it. Religious faith has power over some individuals no less than heroin has control over the addict. Many in our society have their thinking contaminated by prejudices, cultural practices, rituals, class, history and circumstances.

John is a man who holds no ill will toward any other. He approaches almost everything with an open mind; everything, that is, except his religious beliefs. This good man can approach a problem with a calm demeanour, analyse the situation, think about a practical solution and arrive at a reasoned decision.

In spite of all his good sense, he nevertheless believes that Noah could fit all the animals of the earth into a boat. This ark of Noah's was not even big enough to hold all the insects of the world. There are thousands of varieties of beetles alone. Some estimates suggest there are between three hundred and fifty thousand and one million varieties of beetles. Many of these critters eat wood. The Goliath beetle is as big as a man's hand. (It is a wonder how Noah saved the termites and carpenter ants.) Why would such a commonsensical man not approach the religious story of Noah's Ark in the same way as he approaches all else in life?

In the first place, in all other things, he has seen with his own eyes, touched with his own hands, perfected his own intelligence, and has experienced things that grounded him in the natural world. However, when it comes to religion he has seen with other people's eyes (the pastor, his parents, etc.). He has closed his own eyes. His common sense has been perverted, and he permitted religious superstition and supernaturalism to control his thoughts. After all, if you hear only one message, being constantly drilled into you by adults since you were a toddler, you might believe it is true. Professional advertisers know the more you repeat the same message, the more likely people accept it. This may be too simple an explanation as to how this strange thing called religion is able to get a stranglehold on John's sensibilities. How can his brain that produces ideas, born from logic, become so limp and malleable when it turns to religion?

When common sense succumbs to the irrational, normal discourse is impossible. John has good sense in everything else, but when it comes to religion he is wounded. He forms in his head a chaos of thought of which he is afraid to disentangle. He is told that food rained from the sky for forty years, that water turned to wine, that the sea parted upon command, that a snake talks, that a virgin gives birth, and that there is life after death.

These myths violate natural law, contradict science, and fail to correspond with reality or logic. Yet John remains deluded where religion is concerned. He is unable to separate truth from fantasy. He has been infected by *"holy men"* who preach the unbelievable. John, like so many other good people, is gullible. He was brought up since childhood to believe in the Bible. In all other things, common sense governs John's actions. But with religion, John is like a child who believes his older brother when he says, *"Beware of the monster in the dark attic."* Turn on the light. You will see no monster in the attic. As children grow into young adults they discard their belief in the Easter Bunny, Santa Claus and monsters. However, when it comes to religion, they are afraid to turn on the light of reality. They are afraid they may see what they do not want to believe. They may see that there is no god.

John is a good and decent man who has been deluded by religion and adults whom he respected. There are many people like John in this world who are intrinsically good and decent and did not need religion to be so. Deep within each one of us, we all probably believe Mark Twain when he said the following:

"Faith is believing what you know ain't so."

~

Bill's New Car

"A man deluded by unfilled dreams, irrational beliefs or a dogma, clouds his common sense and grasp of reality."
—Brian Hinkley

"No one perceives the world objectively; our senses are contaminated by our hopes."
—Peter A. Ubel

Bill's New Car

Bill is a working man. He makes ends meet and is content with life, even though he had more than his share of hard knocks. He never had much interest in education, or as they called it back then, "book learning." In those days, graduating from high school was an accomplishment. Few of his friends went on to college or even sought higher education. It was an era when you entered the working world as soon as possible.

Bill's parents were killed in a car accident when he was ten years old. From then on, he was raised by his grandmother. His grandmother was religious, and Bill simply accepted his faith without question. He had no other family.

Fresh out of high school, and after working at a few part-time and odd jobs, Bill got a steady job as a shipper at a shovel-making factory. The job paid decent wages. He earned enough to pay the bills and have some fun money, and a little was left over for savings.

Bill's passion was cars. He was known as a backyard mechanic. Everything he knew about cars, he taught himself. He could never afford a new car. He would buy old clunkers and keep them running with gum, wire and duct tape. He had a dream that one day he would have the very best car that was ever made. It would be a car like none other. But that was just a dream.

Bill married his childhood sweetheart two years after graduating from high school. Bill and Sally were in love, and together they built a life. They both wanted children. They tried unsuccessfully for several years. They didn't know if the problem was with Bill or Sally.

They went to church faithfully every Sunday and prayed to God to be blessed with a child. Their prayers were never answered.

Finally, they consulted a doctor, which resulted in many tests. The problem was with Sally's reproductive system. She had difficulty conceiving. When Sally did get pregnant, Bill and Sally were filled with joy. The joy soon turned to disappointment when Sally miscarried. Later on Sally had two more miscarriages.

Further medical advice was sought. The medical costs almost crippled the couple financially. They did, however, manage to hold on to their small house and avoid bankruptcy. As the years passed, they gave up on the thought of ever having a family. They made the best of their life and accepted their situation. Their life together was a good one. The still loved each other and were supportive of one another.

Bill continued to putter around with cars. The financial setback of paying off years of medical bills never allowed Bill to buy a new car. Nonetheless he always longed for a new car. He continued to work at the shovel works for near forty years. By now, he was thinking about retirement. He had built up some nice pension credits, but still wanted to work a few more years. However, rumours were circulating that the shovel business was in trouble, and there was talk about his plant being taken over by another company.

Bill was nervous about the security of his pension. The union told him that his present pension was secure as long as the current ownership remained the same. However, if the plant was bought out, they could not guarantee what would happen to his pension credits.

Bill was eligible for early retirement. He decided to retire early and take his pension.

This decision was a bit stressful for both Bill and Sally, but not near as stressful as the news that would follow. Around the same time Sally wasn't feeling so well. She had made several visits to various doctors. On this day she was told the bad news. She had cancer. It had spread beyond treatment. She had three months to live. How in the world would she tell Bill? She knew Bill was already stressed out about retiring from his job, a decision he didn't really want to make. Now this!

That evening after dinner, Sally sat down with Bill. The air was heavy. Sally; the lovely woman she was, was more upset as to how Bill would deal with this bad news. A more generous person would be hard to find than this gal Sally. She kept thinking how good a man Bill was to her. She thought how many bad hands Bill was dealt; the loss of his mother and father when he was ten; his grandmother, who he found dead on the kitchen floor one day after work; the children she could never give him; leaving a job that he enjoyed; and his dream of a new car that he never realized because of the medical bills.

Sally blamed herself. How was she going to tell this lovely man who always stood by her side? A man she loved so much. Why is life so unfair? she wondered. During the day, as she had thought how she would tell Bill, she reconciled in her mind that it would be a greater wrong not to tell Bill. She told herself that her last three months with Bill would be spent doing all things together. He was retired, and her last moments on this earth would be spent with the man she loved. Just washing dishes or peeling apples together would be the greatest gift Sally could ask for. She rehearsed and replayed over and over in her mind how to tell Bill.

She wanted Bill to feel the same way she was feeling and accept the situation. Sally said to herself, *"If I only have so much time left, I want to make the best of it. I don't want my last days to be sad or gloomy. I want us both to enjoy each other and make every day a precious, happy occasion."*

Sally felt comfortable with her decision. She said to herself, *"I must be strong for Bill's sake."* Sally knew Bill was going to be left all alone. Sally knew Bill would be devastated. They did not have many friends. Their life was quite private and very personal. She understood Bill, and she knew he understood her. They were soul mates.

Sally needed Bill to stand by her one more time and meet this challenge together, just as they had always done before. When Sally broke the news, the reaction was predictable. There were a lot of tears shed that night. But the two were never closer. It was a long evening before sleep would come.

That night in bed was special. They held on to each other all night long. In the morning, they awoke to a warm sunbeam shining through the bedroom window. The sheets and pillowcases were wet from endless crying. Damp tissue paper littered the bedroom floor. Sally and Bill were exhausted but, in a strange way, relieved.

At breakfast, they were quiet. They just looked at each other. For the longest time it seemed they were in some kind of never-never land. It was as though time was suspended. There was no need for talk. Both understood. After breakfast, Bill said, *"Sally, we are going to do exactly as you said. Whatever time we have left together will be the happiest days of our lives."* A big smile came across Sally's face. They embraced.

When they finally breathed a sigh of relief, Sally said, *"When I'm gone I want you to promise me one thing."* *"Yes, of course,"* Bill said. *"I want you to buy that car you always dreamed about,"* Sally said, looking directly into Bill's eyes. Bill hesitated, for just a moment. Then a small delicate smile creased his mouth, and he said, *"OK."*

It was about three months, and many prayers later, that Sally passed away. They had spent this time together just as they had promised each other. For the next several months Bill grieved and endured every human emotion known to man. As he sifted through Sally's belongings, he also sifted through the memories of their life together. It took some time to get back a normal rhythm to his life.

One day, as he was puttering on an old junker, he remembered the promise he made to Sally. He had some savings, but not enough to buy the kind of car he had dreamed about. Regardless, he started visiting car dealerships to check out the latest in automobile technology. On the Internet he spent hours researching his dream car. He was left with an empty feeling in his stomach. Even the best cars seemed to leave him unsatisfied.

Bill, you see, wasn't looking for any ordinary car. He was looking for something that didn't exist, or so he thought. On a repeat visit to one particular dealership, a salesman who Bill had spoken to before approached him. *"Hi, I see you're back,"* said the salesman. *"Can I help you?"* Bill replied, in an exasperated tone, *"Nah, I don't think the car that I am looking for even exists."*

The wily salesman said, *"Trust me, I've always been able to meet everyone's expectations. I think I know what kind of car you are looking for, but first I must ask a few questions."* *"OK,"* Bill said, *"fire away."*

The salesman started, *"You want this car to be all-powerful. The most powerful car that ever existed."* *"Yes,"* said Bill.

"You want this car to be one of a kind. In other words, like no other car out there," the salesman said with confidence. *"Yes, that's exactly what I want,"* said Bill.

"You want this car to be so well built that it will last forever," said the salesman. *"Yes, yes, that's it,"* Bill said with excitement.

"You want this car to have such a presence that people will be in awe of it. So much so that people will both praise it and fear it, right?" said the salesman. Bill's voice began to rise, *"Now you are talking; you know what I really want."*

"Yes, I do, sir, but you can't afford such a car," said the salesman. *"Wait a minute,"* Bill said. *"Look, I have $50,000 in investments."* The salesman laughed. Bill said, *"On top of that, I have another $200,000, if I cash in my retirement plan."* The salesman said, *"Sir, that is indeed a lot of money, but for the kind of car you want, you need a lot more money than that."*

Bill thought for a moment. *"If I sold my house and cashed in all my assets, I could raise $500,000. That's half a million dollars."* The salesman said, *"Come with me."*

The two of them went into a windowless office. The salesman sat down at a very large ornate wooden desk. Nothing was on the desk. The office had no furniture, no pictures on the wall, no cabinets; only the desk and two chairs. The chair behind the desk was a large leather chair. The chair in front of the desk was a simple wooden chair.

The salesman shifted in the leather chair and took from one of the desk drawers a large binder. The binder was embossed with fancy script. It was trimmed with a gold border and had a silk tassel. When the salesman opened the binder, it took up almost half of the desk's surface.

The salesman said, *"In this binder is all the information about your dream car and the terms of the agreement. This is what we promise you. The only things not on this agreement are the purchase price of the car and your signature."*

The binder contained twenty pages of contract language. Bill started to read the contract. It said things like,

- The owner will never need to put oil or fuel into the car.
- No maintenance is ever required.
- Only the owner can talk to this car, and the car will talk to its owner.
- Upon command, the car has a cloaking device to make it invisible to others.
- The car will watch over you, and keep you safe, all the days of your life.
- As long as the owner believes in the car, the car will believe in its owner, and both will have a full and long life.

It went on like this. Bill couldn't believe what he was reading. This car was much more than he had expected. Bill's heart began to pound with excitement. *"I must have this car,"* Bill said. Then, almost immediately, Bill said with suspicion, *"Wait a minute, what does this car look like?"*

"I thought you'd never ask," said the salesman.

The salesman opened the binder to the last page. There was a fancy border around a blank page. *"There is your dream car,"* said the salesman. *"Where?"* said Bill. *"I only see a blank page."* "Oh my," said the salesman, *"I have made a terrible mistake. I have misjudged you entirely."* *"What do you mean?"* said Bill. *"You have had in mind a dream car all your life; is that not so?"* said the salesman. *"Yes,"* said John. The salesman exclaimed, *"You must know what it looks like! You have seen it in your dreams. You have seen it while you were puttering away on those old junkers. You have seen it when daydreaming while sitting on the front porch. You know exactly what it looks like."*

"I want you to concentrate and look at the very centre of the blank page," said the salesman. *"You will see a small red dot. Look at the red dot. Concentrate, concentrate. Do you now see your dream car?"* asked the salesman. *"Yes, yes, I do,"* said Bill, *"It is perfect. It is just what I want."*

Bill left the dealership filled with excitement and anticipation. It was all he could think about over the next few months while he sold his house and cashed in all his assets. He took the half million dollars in a bank draft to the car salesman and signed the agreement. The massive binder was turned over to Bill for his safekeeping and security as proof of purchase. The next day a huge covered truck pulled into Bill's now-rented trailer home.

On the back of the truck was a huge box. The huge box was on a roller mechanism that allowed the box to be placed gently on Bill's driveway. The truck driver said, *"I am told this is your new car. Please sign here for the delivery."*

Bill could hardly contain his excitement as he attacked the big box. Sweat poured from his brow, and his T-shirt was wet from his anticipation. He opened two sides of the big box, and the sunlight exposed its contents.

Bill stood motionless as he stared at the contents of the box. For a few seconds there was not a sound. Then all of a sudden, Bill let out the most blood-curdling scream. His scream was so loud that every resident of the trailer park came running over to see what was wrong. Bill was sitting in a prayer position, but he wasn't praying, he was crying. A resident looked inside the box and said, *"There is nothing in it, only air."*

Epilogue:

Where do we humans get our beliefs from? It seems obvious to many that children are gullible and believe what they are told. But would such be the case with adults? If you want something, or believe in something, with all your heart and all your mind, perhaps you will believe anything.

People will believe what they want to believe. Gods, fairies, elves, angels, trolls, aliens, demons, genies, ghosts and, yes, even dream cars. If you want something strong enough…perhaps you will believe in anything. And there are always those around who will sell you anything.

If we understood our own irrationality and why many people believe the unbelievable, then we might be able to improve the way we think. The sad truth is that we live in an illogical world. Something about the way the human mind works makes people look for a god, for salvation, for eternal life and even an unrealistic dream car that defies rational explanation. Why people believe the illogical is a question that isn't easily explained.

I've come to an uneasy conclusion in my attempt to understand how humans behave. Many people are controlled by emotions, desires, and their wants; others mange to use reason, logic and common sense. Some people allow their heart to dictate their behaviour; others allow their mind. This tug-of-war produces a personal internal conflict of emotion versus reason. In some people emotions will rule. In others reason will win out.

A dream, an unseen heavenly body or belief in the supernatural may begin early in childhood. Maybe for some it is spontaneous, like an epiphany; maybe it is cultural; maybe it is taught; maybe it is all these things and more. Many irrational beliefs can never be eradicated, even through a process of reason. Perhaps humans have innate ways of understanding imaginary things and a need to believe in supernatural forces such that it leads to an acceptance of sacred values, which are essential for human existence.

What a shocking thought for an atheist to postulate!

~

Science v. Religion
or
Nothing Fails Like Prayer

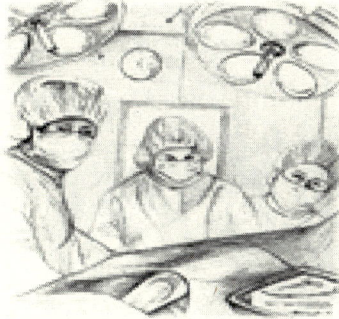

*"If you talk to God, you're religious. If God talks to you —
you're psychotic."*
—Dr. Gregory House (TV Character)

*"And the prayer of faith shall save the sick, and the Lord
shall raise him up; and if he have committed sins, they shall
be forgiven him."*
—James Chapter 5:15

Science v. Religion
or
Nothing Fails Like Prayer

We are well into the twenty-first century, and I often question if the human race has improved over previous generations. I am writing this in the year 2014.

When I was a young boy attending elementary school, we did a class project called *"Life in the Year 2000."* I was around ten years old then, so it was in the mid 1950s. The year 2000 was supposed to be something thrilling. It would be a year when technological advances would meet all of our dreams and fantasies. The world would have been transformed into a type of mystical Oz.

The '50s were filled with the memories, some good, some bad, of the Second World War. Homes had closets and attics full of objects left from the war. I was fascinated by a helmet, a bayonet and my uncle's uniform. I remember the jacket being very heavy and it felt rough to the touch. All of these were keepsakes that remained a constant reminder of past struggles.

At the same time the Korean War was an ominous indication of further world conflicts. It seemed as though the future was a picture of great expectations and further human suffering. This stark ambivalence was a prevailing feature of the times. And yet, one might say, every generation experiences that same tension. We live in a world of contradictions and competing interests. The adventures of space, and the misery of poverty. The advancement of medicine, and the plight of new diseases.

As Charles Dickens wrote in *A Tale of Two Cities*:

"It was the best of times, it was the worst of times, it was the age of wisdom, it was the age of foolishness, it was the epoch of belief, it was the epoch of incredulity, it was the season of Light, it was the season of Darkness, it was the spring of hope, it was the winter of despair, we had everything before us, we had nothing before us, we were all going direct to Heaven, we were all going direct the other way — in short, the period was so far like the present period, that some of its noisiest authorities insisted on its being received, for good or for evil, in the superlative degree of comparison only."

Perhaps it is so that every period of time is the best of times and the worst of times? I want to think that we, as the human race, are becoming better, more caring, more intelligent, and more reasonable. Then again, I see too many examples that, to me, defy reason, defy common sense and seem to propel people into the realm of superstition and illogical belief systems. Theirs is a dogma of the supernatural that can only be described as eerily bizarre.

The older generation was well aware of the devastation of the Great Depression and the war years. They were conservative, reserved and cautious. The younger generation was liberal, less restrained and filled with adventure. The Atomic Age captivated the imagination and fear of the world's population. Bomb shelters, warning sirens and school emergency drills reinforced anxiety over a possible nuclear holocaust. At the same time we were told of the limitless possibilities of the nuclear age. Once again we see the wisdom of Dickens's words.

I remember our class being shown an American television documentary film called **Mr. Sun.** It was filmed in Technicolor! I can still feel and remember the excitement of that word, "Technicolor." It seems rather mundane and juvenile today that anyone would be excited over Technicolor.

It was written, produced, and directed by Frank Capra. The film explains how the Sun works and how it also plays a huge part in human life. It was first televised by CBS in 1956. The film marked the last project of Lionel Barrymore, who played the voice of Father Time.

It was a combination of real-life sequences interspersed with animation. It was geared towards young children growing up in the nuclear age. One would think that the nuclear age was going to bring us an endless supply of inexpensive, clean, nuclear power that would herald the age of plenty for all of humankind. The young were optimistic about the future. The film ends with Dr. Research and Father Time providing an overview explaining that human curiosity has helped drive scientific achievements and how important it is to ask questions of both science and religion.

Following the viewing of *Mr. Sun*, all of the children came away with dreams of a futuristic world filled with peace, harmony and scientific inventions that would transform our current world into a paradise.

Each of us was given instructions to draw a picture of the world in the year 2000. The picture could represent a new invention of whatever we wished. We would then make a verbal presentation about our thoughts on the year 2000 and explain our drawing. I remember it only too well.

Every one of the boys and girls displayed a positive picture of the future. Many of the scientific predictions represented by the students have in fact come true. We are, however, still waiting on the flying car to relieve congestion on our highways.

When you are young, you do believe anything is possible. You dream of things that seem impractical. Your imagination is unrestrained. Thank goodness for the inspiration of the young. Age and time have a way of curbing a person's enthusiasm. Experience can be a teacher. It can also make one cautious and doubtful and become cynical. When one is slapped down, or subjected to negative criticism, or told not to question authority, the drive toward new horizons becomes a remote goal. Blind obedience drains energy away from curiosity and adventure — a necessary aspect that helps to create the excitement of discovery.

Well, the year 2000 has come and gone. Was it a magical year? Hardly! No more magical than 1999, 1956 or 2014. It was just another year in the history of the human race.

I am left to question and ponder the following: *"What advances society? Who advances society? Why bother to advance society?"*

In any discussion of this nature there is always the gadfly or annoying person who will pose an irritating question rather than pose a critical or positive query. His/her aim is not to seek clarification but rather to stir the pot for no other reason than to be obnoxious. The gadfly will say, *"What does it mean to 'advance'?"* Maybe your understanding of advancement is not mine. You see, we will always have those who have been sprayed with pixie dust.

Ignore them not, but tolerate them with a pinch of salt. For these folks live in a world of unexplained wonderment that is part of the human psyche. It is a burden the rest of us must bear. So here is the pinch of salt for those afflicted by the effects of pixie dust.

By "advance," I mean progress, betterment, improving the human condition, a higher quality of life, better human relations, alleviating suffering, improving understanding, moving forward instead of back to the days of polio, small pox, the black plague, no electricity, etc. It means the enhancement and protection of life's beauty, nature, the environment and the sensitive use and care of all the creatures and resources of the world for the benefit of all humankind. Perhaps most important, a way to prevent human annihilation and safeguard the little blue dot that is our home in the vastness of the Cosmos.

If this is not understood, I can do no more for the annoying folks who are suffering from this pixie dust affliction.

The second list of questions comprises the counterpoints: *"What retards society? Who retards society?"* and most compelling, *"Why retard society?"*

I know the word "retard" is politically incorrect. The gadfly will often use the straw dog tactic to deflect those who wish to pursue constructive discussion. "Retard" is meant purely as one would find it in the dictionary. That is, to hinder, to hold back, to delay, to frustrate, or to impede. Who therefore are those who would, because of their dogma, impede the advancement of society?

In this discussion many folks will see varying shades of grey. To be sure, not all in life is black and white.

History, science, facts, evidence and reason can produce a clear and unequivocal picture of the truth — a truth beyond all doubt. Did I say "all doubt"? As we shall see, there is practically never a time, situation or circumstance that removes all doubt.

Let us examine an example. A religious couple have a two-year-old baby named Emily. All of a sudden, Emily becomes sick. The couple take their child to their pastor, who encourages the couple to pray to God for divine intervention to cure the child. The three of them spend day and night praying for a miraculous recovery for the child.

In a couple of days, several members of their church attend the couple's home to pray. The whole group set up a system of around-the-clock praying in shifts. The child is never alone for one second. There is always someone or several people circling the baby's crib, praying to God, appealing to this invisible creature in the sky to heal the sick child.

Following a week of praying, the child deteriorates. The child turns blue and gasps for air. The mother, in a panic, orders her husband to drive Emily to the hospital. Emily is rushed to the emergency room. The onsite doctor says the baby needs an immediate operation, or the child will surely die. The parents consent to the operation.

During the operation, the child's parents, along with their pastor and several members of the church's congregation, pray in the waiting room. After three hours of surgery, the doctor emerges. One can tell, by the doctor's expression, that the news is not encouraging.

The doctor says, *"Your baby was very sick. If she was brought in to us three or four days ago, her chances of survival would have been excellent. We have done everything possible, but I am sorry to say her chances of recovery are extremely unlikely."*

The mother cries uncontrollably. She pleads with the doctor to come pray with them. The doctor replies, *"Madam, I mean no disrespect, but don't you think you've done enough praying?"*

Two hours later, the child succumbs to her illness. Two weeks later, the doctor is sued by the child's parents for ten million dollars. They claim, among other things, in the motion before the courts that the doctor was unsympathetic, demonstrated a lack of professional concern, and did not conduct the surgery in the best possible way to save the child. They claim the doctor was prejudiced against them because of their religious beliefs.

I am sure the reader would like to know what happened during the trial and the final outcome. However, this is not the purpose of this story.

I am left to ask the questions posed earlier. Does religion and praying advance society and the human condition? How did religion and praying help poor little Emily? One is tempted to write off this incident as an isolated, one-of-a-kind matter relegated to a small fanatical religious sect. When one examines the religious beliefs, customs, rituals and dogma of all the major religions, it becomes frightening.

Though 80 percent of the world's population claim to be religious, one can be thankful that only a small percentage actually strictly adheres to their own religious preaching.

Fundamentalists, orthodoxy, extremism and fanatics do, in fact, influence millions in our society.

During the operation, it was ironic that the team of nurses and assistants who helped the doctor included one who was a member of the same religious sect as the family. This member of the operating team confided in the mother. She told the mother that the doctor was frustrated and expressed his anger over the stupidity of these religious morons who would allow their daughter to reach this state before seeking medical attention.

At the trial, this member of the operating team testified against the doctor. The trial judge in this case happened to be a religious fundamentalist. What do you think was the judge's decision?

~

Epilogue

The story you just read is fictional. However, there are many true-life accounts of similar stories that occur all over the world. As you read further, you will find a verbatim article that appeared in the December 2, 2014, edition of the *Hamilton Spectator* from Hamilton, Ontario, Canada.

Victor J, Stenger in his book entitled *God and the Folly of Faith: The Incompatibility of Science and Religion*, on page 288, wrote the following:

"And what about the negative impact that religion has on health? Between 1975 and 1995, at least 172 children in the United States die, perhaps 140 of medically curable illness, because their parents refused them medical treatment for religious reasons...."

"While those numbers are not large, every child is significant, and many more children are harmed by the lack of immunizations and other refusals by religious parents to provide modern medical treatments and preventative measures. Parents are allowed to do this because of unconscionable religious exemptions in child-abuse prevention laws. It should be noted that anti-vaccination affects everyone, not just the unfortunate children of religious fanatics."

How strong is the belief in prayer among the religious? I have lifted from this website the following Bible passages. (http://www.openbible.info/topics/prayer_for_healing)

James 5:14-16 ESV *Is anyone among you sick? Let him call for the elders of the church, and let them pray over him, anointing him with oil in the name of the Lord. And the prayer of faith will save the one who is sick, and the Lord will raise him up.*

And if he has committed sins, he will be forgiven. Therefore, confess your sins to one another and pray for one another, that you may be healed. The prayer of a righteous person has great power as it is working.

Mark 10:27 ESV Jesus looked at them and said, *"With man it is impossible, but not with God. For all things are possible with God."*

Philippians 4:6 ESV *Do not be anxious about anything, but in everything by prayer and supplication with thanksgiving let your requests be made known to God.*

3 John 1:2 ESV *Beloved, I pray that all may go well with you and that you may be in good health, as it goes well with your soul.*

Matthew 10:1 ESV *And he called to him his twelve disciples and gave them authority over unclean spirits, to cast them out, and to heal every disease and every affliction.*

Mark 16:18 ESV *They will pick up serpents with their hands; and if they drink any deadly poison, it will not hurt them; they will lay their hands on the sick, and they will recover.*

Now it is time to believe the unbelievable. Read the following verbatim article from the *Hamilton Spectator*, and be prepared to enter the **Twilight Zone**.

Family expected corpse to be resurrected

Wife pleads to Corner's Act charge after leaving husband's body in home for six months

WARNING: GRAPHIC CONTENT – MOLLY HAYES, The Hamilton Spectator

---

Peter Wald's family truly believed he would rise from the dead.

They believed it because they had prayed for it, every single day, while his corpse lay rotting for six months in an upstairs bedroom of their Hamilton home.

When neighbours asked about her husband, curious about the 52 year-old man's seeming disappearance, Kaling Wald would tell them he was "in Gods hands now."

On Monday, Kaling, 50, pleaded guilty to failing to notify police or the coroner that her husband had died due to a sickness that was not being treated by a doctor. It's the first known case of its kind (involving the resurrection belief) in Canada.

The criminal charges originally laid in the case – neglect of duty regarding a dead body and offering an indignity to a body – were withdrawn and replaced with that single charge under the Coroner's Act.

Kaling had no ill intent, all agreed. As assistant Crown attorney Janet Booy put it, the devout Christian woman's faith had "tainted and warped her better judgement."

"We were trusting God…we thought, ok Lord, you know better." Kaling told The Spectator after court Monday.

Kaling's lawyer Peter Boushy described the case as one of "over-exuberant faith."

Peter Wald, 52, died "probably around March 20th" last year, according to the agreed statement of facts read out in court Monday. He'd suffered from diabetes and his left foot had become infected. But he had refused to go to the hospital and believed God would cure him.

He went into a coma, she says, and days later she noticed his stomach bloating and signs of rigor mortis on his forehead.

She then left him – his body covered with two blankets, his head with a toque – in bed and padlocked the bedroom door.

Kaling sealed in the door and the vents with duct tape to protect her family from the smell of the cadaver.

And then for six months, life went on and they prayed for their dead husband and father in the bed upstairs as they awaited his return.

It was September 17, 2013 when the body was finally discovered. The sheriff had arrived to evict the family from the St. Matthews Avenue house, near Barton Street East and Wentworth Street North, after they had defaulted on the mortgage.

Expecting the eviction, the family packed the dead man's belongings and had his shoes and bags ready to go.

"That was how strong our faith was," Kaling says.

But when she unlocked the bedroom door his body, which had attracted rodents, was so decomposed it was impossible to identify by photograph.

His feet were sticking out from under the blankets with gauze still wrapped around the left foot.

"He (the sheriff) said, OK that's enough, close the door," Wald remembers.

Police and the coroner was called, but because of the mummified state of his body toxicology tests could not be conducted and a cause of death was not confirmed – though it's "likely due to natural causes," the pathologist's report says.

The Niagara Children's Aid Society was called in as well, but found no concerns for the well-being of the couple's children and the case was closed.

Everyone living in the home – Kaling, five of her six children age 11 to 22, and seven other friends – were interviewed by police. Each provided a consistent account of his death and their religious belief that he could be resurrected.

In court Monday, the Crown acknowledged that had the case gone to trial their chance at a conviction would be slim. There was no criminal intent – as Wald said afterwards, she wasn't even aware there was a law against not reporting the body.

"It's an extremely sad case….she truly believed her husband was going to be resurrected from the dead, even after six month," said Booy.

Booy says she researched the law extensively and could not find another case like this.

Kaling, who has no past criminal record, had her sentence suspended and was put on 18 months of probation and ordered to seek counselling around the "public health concerns" of the incident.

"Your belief that your husband would resurrect is not an issue," Superior Court Justice Marjoh Agro said at her plea Monday. "This is not about your religious beliefs. It is about your safety, the safety of your children and the safety of the community at large."

The Walds were known around their neighbourhood for their blue minivan that was covered in messages of love for God, and had crosses carved into the headlights so they would project the religious symbol.

They were regularly spreading the gospel and handing out food for homeless people in the winter through their street ministry, Wald says.

She disputes references in the media that the family was seen chanting in the backyard and says they were simply putting on religious skits for homeless people in the neighbourhood.

The family has since moved to Fort Erie. With the criminal case behind her, she says she can finally grieve the loss of her husband and move past the attention the strange case received.

"It was unusual, yes. It was certainly not normal, and we won't do that again…laws exist and we know that now."

But she still believes strongly in resurrection, and says there have been many "documented" cases of it around the world. Her faith was not shaken by the legal consequences, she says.

"In fact it has cast me more at the mercy of God, because He is the ultimate judge."

"When one person suffers from a delusion, it is called insanity. When many people suffer from a delusion it is called a Religion."

— **Robert M. Pirsig,** *Zen and the Art of Motorcycle Maintenance*

World's Greatest Killers

"If you think you've got an inside track to absolute truth, you become doctrinaire, humourless and intellectually constipated. The greatest crimes in history have been perpetrated by such religious and political and racial fanatics, from the persecutions of the Inquisition on down to Communist purges and Nazi genocide."

—Saul Alinsky

World's Greatest Killers

There is much debate about the topic of the great killers. Those who immediately try to answer this question think of folks like the Boston Strangler, Jeffrey Dahmer, Ted Bundy and a host of others.

Yet the evil deeds committed by these psychopaths pale in comparison to the recorded history of other killers, some of them long forgotten. Others, people may have never heard of or thought of as a killer.

One evening, an old history professor and two of his top university students got together over beer to have a friendly discussion on this rather morbid topic, they, of course, being, shall we say, interested in history. Why not the history of killers? They approached the matter in a composed and detached manner.

The old professor, now in his late sixties, was always a rebel of sorts. He is a product of the '60s social revolution and an admirer of Saul Alinsky. His name is John Richards, but most of his students have forgotten his real name, and they affectionately refer to him as JR. His classes are one of the most popular on campus. He has a knack for engaging his students, creating controversy and making everyone think, including the university's administration, board of directors and alumni.

He has long been suspected of being an atheist, but some of his detractors have been unable to successfully smear him with this tag, although not for lack of trying. JR kept his religious beliefs to himself. He taught his students how to think, not what to think.

Peter, one of JR's A students, who was part of this beer-drinking discussion, came from a devout Catholic family. Peter was a committed Christian, and his parents had hoped he would, someday, enter the priesthood. While Peter steadfastly and unabashedly wore his religious beliefs on his sleeve, he was also open-minded and unusually curious, much to his credit.

The final member of this triumvirate was Cecil. Cecil was in the classical sense…a "nerd." His dedication to studying most any topic was more than an obsession; it was his mission in life to know everything there is to know. He would talk about any subject, anywhere, anytime, any place. Analytical discussion and debate coursed through his blood stream as surely as did white and red corpuscles.

JR chose a corner table in a local bohemian watering hole, suitable for this type of semi-inebriated discussion. The stage was set for what was about to be an unforgettable evening. The waiter plopped in front of the motley three a pitcher of cold beer, accompanied by three frosty mugs. The atmosphere was perfect for this exercise in intellectual masturbation. However, before the games began, JR explained the parameters of the topic and his role. He would act as a facilitator, rather than a full participant.

JR said, *"We need to identify not only the world's greatest killers but also the most monstrous, insidious, inhumane and callous rotten bastards you can think of."*

Cecil couldn't wait to spark the debate. He exclaimed, *"I know you two are going to suggest some other despicable characters, but this particular lowlife personally destroyed the lives of untold numbers of children."*

He went on to describe the revolting deeds of a fellow no longer talked about much — in fact, he's almost forgotten. This monster is Gilles de Rais, a French nobleman born in 1404. The precise number of Rais's victims is not known, as most of the bodies were burned or buried. The number of murders is generally placed between eighty and two hundred; a few have conjectured numbers upwards of six hundred. Most of his victims were young children, and how he treated those innocents would make a lumberjack cry. Cecil choked up and had difficulty describing some of the horrid details.

Cecil proceeded to describe some of the most horrific actions known to mankind. The children were violated, mutilated and tortured to death. When he finished his story, Cecil took a swig of beer then sat back and relaxed.

"Whew," Peter sighed, as he looked at JR., who said, *"Don't look at me; see if you can top that."* Peter started, *"As horrible and monstrous as this French nobleman was, his killings barely scratch the surface. Let's get to the real killers."* Peter described in disgusting detail how the Communist dictator Pol Pot tortured, starved and executed the ordinary and simple people of Cambodia. Anyone and everyone who was hinted to be an obstacle or slight hindrance to Pol Pot's iron rule was eliminated, and the methods used were among the most inhumane that the world has ever known.

Peter described how hundreds of thousands of people were taken out in shackles to dig their own mass graves. Then the Khmer Rouge (Pol Pot's soldiers) buried them alive. A Khmer Rouge extermination prison directive ordered, *"Bullets are not to be wasted."* Peter said, *"These mass graves are often referred to as The Killing Fields."*

Some of Peter's Christian friends had related stories to him as to how the Khmer Rouge classified people by religion and ethnic group. They banned all religions and dispersed minority groups, forbidding them to speak their languages or to practise their customs. They especially targeted Buddhist monks, Muslims, Christians, Western-educated intellectuals, educated people in general, people who had contact with Western countries or with Vietnam, disabled people, and the ethnic Chinese, Laotians and Vietnamese.

Some were put in the infamous S-21 camp for interrogation and torture, as to obtain confessions useful to the government. Many others were summarily executed. Peter's Christian friends told him about the torture system at S-21 and how it was designed to make prisoners confess to whatever crimes they had been charged with by their captors.

Peter said, *"Prisoners were routinely beaten and tortured with electric shocks, searing hot metal instruments and hanging, as well as through the use of various other devices. Some prisoners were cut with knives or suffocated with plastic bags. Other methods for generating confessions included pulling out fingernails while pouring alcohol on the wounds, holding prisoners' heads under water, and the use of the waterboarding technique."*

Both JR and Cecil remained totally silent as Peter verbally drew a picture of the horrific torture scenes. JR remained stoic. Cecil was mesmerized.

Peter continued to tell in explicit detail how females were sometimes raped by their interrogators, even though sexual abuse was against government policy. Some perpetrators were found out and executed. But many interrogators were never disciplined, and thousands of prisoners died from this kind of abuse.

A special "Medical Unit" killed at least one hundred prisoners by bleeding them to death. Medical experiments were performed on certain prisoners. Inmates were sliced open and organs removed with no anaesthetic. Others were attached to intravenous pumps and every drop of blood was drained from their bodies to see how long they could survive. The most difficult prisoners were skinned alive.

Peter hesitated for a moment, took a deep breath, and said, *"As far as mass killers and exterminators of human beings; Some say Pol Pot was responsible for the extermination of three million people, approximately 25 percent of the population of Cambodia — now we are talking real numbers."* Peter seemed relieved to have finished telling his story.

Both JR and Cecil were impressed with the detail with which Peter was able to expound upon the atrocities committed by Pol Pot. Cecil was not all that eager to respond immediately. He waived to the waiter. The waiter arrived and asked, "Are you ready to order now?" Cecil said, rather sheepishly, *"I'm not hungry right now; just bring us another pitcher of beer."* A small snicker was heard from JR.

With the trio's beer mugs refilled, Cecil was ready to respond. He congratulated Peter on such a well-researched presentation and was a bit nervous as whether he could adequately counter Peter's masterful depiction of reprehensible cruelty.

With steely determination, he resolved he would not be outdone. He shouted, *"Stalin!"* A couple from another table was startled at the outburst and glared at the assembly of three. An uncomfortable Cecil could have crawled under the table. He was momentarily embarrassed, as it was most uncommon for Cecil to have such a lapse of discipline.

He shook off his discomfort and continued to explain why Joseph Stalin, the Soviet Union dictator, deserves to beat out Pol Pot for the title of the "World's Greatest Killer." Cecil started on a long diatribe lasting fifteen minutes. It was indeed a remarkable feat of never-ending verbosity.

One could swear he never stopped to take a breath as he expounded at length upon each of Stalin's depraved acts. When Cecil had finished, he had thoroughly covered Stalin's hundreds of thousands of purges and executions; the over 3.3 million people deported to Siberia or various hostile countries, where most died of starvation, malnutrition or disease; the over 18 million that were imprisoned, sent to gulags or placed into forced labour camps, most of whom died a torturous and miserable death; and the 5 to 10 million Soviet citizens who were deliberately placed into an enforced famine.

It appeared that Cecil had completed his list of abhorrent killings conducted by this miscreant, when suddenly he remembered the attempted genocide of the Ukraine where between four and five million Ukrainians suffered a shameful and atrocious death at the hands of Stalin's second enforced famine. Stalin was partial to starvation for his victims.

Cecil concluded by saying, *"In all; this Soviet monster was responsible for the gruesome killing of some seventeen to twenty million people. A few researchers place the number much higher."*

Peter sat with his head in his left hand while his fingers rubbed his reddened eyes. He took off his glasses and placed them on the table in front of him. He clasped his hands together and looked at both JR and Cecil straight in their eyes, and sadly asked, *"Why is there so much cruelty in this world of ours?"*

JR, who had remained uncharacteristically quiet most of the evening said, *"You two are students of history. It is important that historians document and record these events so that this generation and generations that follow know and understand the folly of our descendants' behaviour. It can only be hoped that your teachings may help prevent similar sordid acts in the future."*

Peter said, *"I think I need another beer."* JR, in trying to ease the emotional atmosphere, reminded his two students that they are scholars and soon-to-be authorities. *"Therefore one must approach the subject dispassionately,"* chimed JR. *"Now go to it, Peter. You are at bat,"* demanded JR.

Peter said, *"There is no doubt that Stalin was one rotten son of a bitch, but he wasn't the worst."* Not to be outdone, Peter said, *"I really don't need to tell you about the Nazi cruelty and Hitler's megalomaniac obsession to conquer the world."* Peter went on to elaborate about Hitler's atrocities; Hitler's actions have been recorded more accurately than perhaps any other despot's in history. *"Is it really necessary for me to enumerate in explicit detail the monstrosity of this reprehensible Fascist dictator?"* queried Peter. The question was as much rhetorical as anything else. It was as though JR and Cecil were ready to concede to Peter, as they logically knew where Peter was heading.

Peter said, *"In terms of number of deaths, it is debateable who was responsible for more deaths, Stalin or Hitler. Both of these monsters rank high on the list of the world's greatest killers. Between bombs, the military invasions of many countries, concentration camps, mass firing squads, and the chilling gas chambers, this little imp with the funny moustache can take credit for some nineteen million people being executed, murdered or tortured to death."*

"Why do I make the claim that Hitler is worse than Stalin? It is because of the Holocaust," Peter cried. *"This attempt to commit genocide on an entire race and wipe out the Jewish people from the face of the earth has got to be considered pure evil. Maybe Stalin was just as evil as Hitler, but we have clear evidence that Hitler's cruelty would never have stopped unless the world's allies joined together to stop this evil against humanity."* Peter then raised his glass and said, *"Thank God he was stopped, or the world would indeed be a much different, but not better, place in which to live."*

At that, JR cleared his throat and said, *"Peter, I don't think God had much to do with stopping Hitler. Perhaps you were right when you said the world's allies were the ones."*

At that, Cecil just grinned.

It appeared, for a moment that the discussion had come to its conclusion. Surely old Adolph is the all-time champion killer. He must be the world's most efficient, if not monstrous, killer of humankind. Yes, there appeared to be no doubt about it. Hitler wins the title.

JR mused for a moment, *"You know, you both have done a good job here, but I think you have missed one modern day monster that many in the Western world seem to forget."* Cecil thought just for a split second and then burst out, *"What's that, you say? You are talking about Mao Ze-Dong."* JR replied, *"Yes, indeed. Chairman Mao, better known as simply Mao, has quite an enviable record that any self-respecting killer would be proud to proclaim."*

"So, Cecil," JR intoned, *"why don't you tell us about Mao's killing prowess?"*

Cecil paused and then struggled for a moment. *"Well, this is not an area where I have done a lot of study, but I think I know what you are getting at."*

At that instance Cecil recalled reading a research paper on Mao that he had never needed to use before now. It started to come back to him. *"Yes, yes, I know what kind of hell existed in China under Mao's iron hand. But as I recall,"* said Cecil, *"China was already in such a mess with a variety of cruel leaders, civil wars and Japanese invaders and all sorts of other problems, that Mao is viewed as a liberator by millions of Chinese."*

Cecil started out by saying there are two sides to the story of Mao. He was definitely a ruthless killer. Cecil went on to describe what he remembers reading about Mao's life.

This is what Cecil remembered. According to the authoritative *Black Book of Communism,* an estimated sixty-five million Chinese died as a result of Mao's repeated, merciless attempts to create a new "communist" China. Anyone who got in his way was done away with — by execution, imprisonment or forced famine.

For Mao, the number-one enemy was the intellectual. In fact, he boasted how his Great Proletarian Cultural Revolution buried alive forty-six thousand scholars.

The most inhumane example of Mao's contempt for human life came when he ordered the collectivization of China's agriculture under the ironic slogan "the *Great Leap Forward.*" A deadly combination of lies about grain production, disastrous farming methods (profitable tea plantations, for example, were turned into rice fields), and misdistribution of food produced the worst famine in human history.

Deaths from hunger reached more than 50 percent in some Chinese villages. The total number of dead from famine alone was between thirty and forty million.

A radical group of students who worshipped Mao were given free rein, with Mao's blessing, to terrorize and root out anyone who spoke against the Cultural Revolution. Their numbers grew and seemed to be answerable to no one.

Professors were dressed in grotesque clothes and dunce caps, their faces smeared with ink. They were then forced to get down on all fours and bark like dogs. Some were beaten to death, some even eaten — all for the promulgation of Maoism. A reluctant Mao finally called in the Red Army to put down the marauding Red Guards when they began attacking Communist Party members, but not before one million Chinese died.

All the while, Mao kept expanding the one thousand forced labour camps throughout China. Fifty million Chinese passed through the Chinese version of the Soviet gulag. Twenty million died as a result of the primitive living conditions and fourteen-hour work days.

Such calculated cruelty exemplified Mao's philosophy: *"Political power grows out of the barrel of a gun."*

From 1949 to 1969 how many people were slaughtered? Some say fifty million to seventy-eight million, with most researchers settling on sixty-five million people.

And yet, Mao Zedong remains the most honoured figure in the Chinese Communist Party. At one end of historic Tiananmen Square is Mao's mausoleum, visited daily by large, respectful crowds. At the other end of the square is a giant portrait of Mao above the entrance to the Forbidden City, the favourite site of visitors, Chinese and foreign.

So really there's a bit of a gap when it comes to modern Chinese history.

"Instead of 'How many people died because of Chairman Mao,' I remember," Cecil said, *"something about 'How many people lived because of Chairman Mao?' If it's reasonable to attribute all unnatural deaths in China since 1949 to this one man, then surely it's also reasonable to attribute all life beyond the 1949 life expectancy to the same man!"*

Cecil pondered, *"One is left to question, how could the world sit idly by and allow such mass exterminations? How could such human destruction take place? It seems Mao employed mass starvation, forced labour and executions; that ranks him the number-one all-time best killer in human history. In fact, they even came up with a new name for it. They call it 'democide.'"* *"What is democide?"* asked Peter. *"I've heard of genocide, but what is democide?"*

Cecil replied, *"Democide is a term revived and redefined by the political scientist R. J. Rummel as 'the murder of any person or people by their government, including genocide, politicide and mass murder.'"*

"Well, that closes the book on this debate. It appears the fat Chinese dictator Mao is the world's historical leading killer at up to seventy-eight million slaughtered souls," said Peter.

JR was quite proud of both his students and told them how impressed he was with their knowledge of history. He congratulated them on being able to quote statistics and recall certain details of atrocities committed. He said, *"Before you make up your mind on this question, I want you to consider something else."*

"What do you mean?" asked Cecil. *"Figures can lie, and liars can figure, so I'm going to do a little figuring of my own,"* said JR. *"When did you say Mao did all this killing?"*

Cecil replied, *"Well, mostly from 1949 to 1969."*

"Hmm," JR wondered. *"I figure the population of the world was between two and four billion people in this twenty-year period."* *"So what?"* responded Cecil. *"SO WHAT?"* replied JR in an unusually abrupt manner. JR explained, *"Look, my friend, this Mao fellow had a lot more to work with than some other historical figures. Go back say one thousand years in history. Do you think the folks back then had guns, bullets, mortar and bombs, tanks and planes?"*

"What do you think the population of the world was one thousand years ago?" asked JR. *"Oh, I don't know, maybe about four hundred million,"* replied Cecil. *"Close enough,"* said JR, *"four hundred million compared to four billion is quite a spread...and Mao's China had a very large portion of that four billion."*

"Now go back one thousand years. Can you think of a monstrous killer that almost conquered most of the world in those days?" asked JR. *"Do you mean Genghis Khan?"* asked Cecil.

"Right again, my good man," said JR. He continued, *"I want you to imagine the one thousand years' advantage Mao had over old Khan. Years of advanced technology and learned techniques on how to mass exterminate citizens was a big advantage for Mao over poor old Khan who had to rely on horses, spears and swords."*

"Gee, I guess you make a good point there," said Peter. *"OK, both of you, I want you to tell me what you know about Genghis Khan,"* stated JR.

The two put their heads together, wanting to impress their professor, and produced the following facts based upon their knowledge and study of the Great Khan. Apparently no one in the entire ancient OR modern history conquered as much territory as Genghis Khan. Between 1206 and his death in 1227, the Mongol leader Genghis Khan conquered nearly twelve million square miles of territory — that is the combined size in area of the United States of America, Canada and China.

Along the way, he cut a merciless path through Asia and Europe that left untold millions dead, but he also modernized Mongolian culture, embraced religious freedom and helped open contact between East and West. He was a ruthless ruler who was equal parts military genius, political statesman and bloodthirsty terror.

While it's impossible to know for sure how many people perished during the Mongol conquests, many historians put the number around forty million. Censuses from the Middle Ages show that the population of China plummeted by tens of millions during the Khan's lifetime, and scholars estimate that he may have killed a full three-fourths of modern-day Iran's population during his war with the Khwarezmid Empire. All told, the Mongols' attacks may have reduced the entire world population by as much as 11 percent. Compared to World War II, the deadliest military conflict in history, when over sixty million people were killed, this was over 3 percent of the world population.

Cecil exclaimed, *"Ha ha! Moa is the best killer. He did away with seventy-eight million, almost twice as many."* Peter interjected, *"Yes, but don't forget the population was ten times smaller and Moa had a thousand-year edge on old Genghis."*

"Well now, I suppose when you take all of this into consideration I guess we must concede that Ghengis Khan wins the title," said Cecil. Peter agreed.

"Not so fast," JR piped up. *"I think you forgot one more historical figure that outdid all of these rotten bastards."* JR asked Peter, *"Do you believe in the Bible?"* *"Yes,"* replied Peter. *"Do you believe there is a God?"* asked JR. *"But of course,"* said Peter. *"What about you, Cecil?"* Cecil replied, *"Oh, I don't know. I don't think about such things very much. I suppose there is a God."*

"Well, let's just assume for a moment there is a God and everything in the Bible is true," JR suggested. JR continued and presented a proposition. He suggested the two examine some historical facts a little more closely. For instance, he suggested that the population figures of the ancient world and the modern world be compared. JR said, *"Let's look at the facts, as best we know them."*

JR suggested that if you have a larger population, you have the benefit of being able to kill a lot more people. If you have a smaller population, you can only kill so many. So your natural resources are limited. Both Cecil and Peter agreed. They said to JR, *"Alright, so make your point."*

JR was prepared in advance and had his two apprentices examine the population of the world from 10,000 BC to present day, say 2011. JR produced a chart that, according to world population analysts, looked something like this.

10,000 BC.......2.5 million

5,000 BC........18 million

1,000 BC........115 million

Year 1..........300 million

1,000 AD.......310 million

1,500 AD.........0.5 billion
1,900 AD.........1.6 billion
1950 AD..........2.5 billion
2011 AD..........7 billion

"So what?" Peter shouted. *"Sooooooooooo...between 10,000 BC to Year +1 there were only a few million people to work with. This was a time when begetting and smiting prevailed, according to the Bible. It was tough having all the begetting keep up with all the smiting. And there sure was a lot of smiting taking place,"* clarified JR.

"What are you trying to say?" Peter asked with his voice rising. *"All I am saying is, if there is a god and the Bible is truly the word of God, then as historians we must examine the claims as though they are true and factual accounts of history. If not, then we must dismiss it altogether,"* explained JR.

Peter accepted JR's reasoning purely as an academic exercise. JR continued and presented information as was written in the Bible. He wanted to challenge his two students, whose history studies did not include the Bible.

JR presented the following:
"As it is written in the Bible, and we know everything in the Bible is true, because after all it is God's word. In fact, God himself committed or commanded a whole lot of smiting. He got so pissed off with his people that he kept killing them off. At one time he wiped everyone off the face of the earth with a flood, save and except Noah and his family. A mere eight folks were left after the biggest one-time killing of all life in the history of the world. At least, that's what we are told. Since millions of people believe this to be true, well, that makes it true. Doesn't it?" asked JR.

This was a rhetorical question, and JR wasn't really looking for a response. JR gave his students some more to think about it.

Given the population of the times, it is estimated that God, either by himself or on his command, wiped out some twenty-five million people. Not too shabby a record considering he only had a few million folks to work with. It was no wonder the population didn't grow much in the early years. God just kept killing them off soon after they were begetted. It's pretty hard to keep a population growing when the killings exceed the begetting.

If God ordered up another world flood today, that would be seven billion people he could drown in one swipe. Not to mention all the animals, plants, vegetation, butterflies and birds.

JR went on to describe in vivid detail the killing by God or ordered by God in the following:

- All the plagues upon Egypt: approximately 1 million plus.
- A seven year famine: 70,000
- Sodom and Gomarrah: 2,000
- The slaughter of the Midianites: 200,000
- Og and all the men, women and children: 60,000
- Gideons conquests: 120,000
- King David: at least 500,000
- God kills about 200,000 Syrians
- An angel from God kills about 185,000

At this point, Peter had had enough. *"Where did you get all of these statistics?"* Peter asked. *"It's right there in the Bible,"* replied JR. *"Have you ever read the Bible?"* Asked JR. *"Well, of course,"* said Peter.

"All of the Bible?" asked JR. *"Well, maybe not all of it,"* replied Peter. *"Perhaps you should take the time to read all of it, and you can start with the following passages,"* suggested JR. JR proceeded to provide a list of passages that Peter may not have heard in church.

"If the Bible is true, the evidence is compelling," said JR. JR proceeded to read various Bible passages from the "Good Book" that he had brought along with him just for the occasion.

Following ten more minutes of some of the most monstrous, hideous and unconscionable acts known to the history of man, JR was able to show both Peter and Cecil just what kind of demented killer this God of the Bible actually was.

Peter was astounded. *"Why, I didn't realize such passages existed – I've never heard of these things before,"* protested Peter. *"Of course not,"* JR replied. Cecil, rather dumbfounded, remained silent. JR said, *"Many religious leaders simply do not tell their parishioners about God's vengeful and hateful behaviour."*

JR demonstrated that God, for a period of three to four thousand years went on a maniacal killing spree. Some years before the arrival of Christ, God eased off the killings. It was a record that clearly demonstrated that God, both personally as well as by ordering others, slaughtered newborn babies, innocent children and millions upon millions of people, including all of nature's lovely creatures. These actions were done in fits of hatred and malicious anger. So horrific was God's spiteful wrath that he became the epic killer of all those who are in the Killer's Hall of Shame. All the dictators and evil leaders in the history of the world could not match God's psychopathic and sociopathic behaviour.

This was done at a time when the world's population was in the few millions, not the billions we have today. Based upon the evidence, the facts as presented in the Bible, the testimony of those who have studied and stand by the word of God, as well as God's own testimony to his crimes against humanity, the verdict is now rendered.

"God is indeed great...as the Muslims often say," said JR. As JR looked at his two students, he said, *"I am not making this up...it is all right here in the Bible. In my opinion, God is by far the all-time world's leading killer of humankind of anyone in the history of the world."*

Peter seemed quite upset over this revelation and looked uncomfortably conflicted. Cecil didn't know what to think. The turn of events were unexpected and left both somewhat unsettled.

JR said, *"Look, gents, I didn't mean to upset you, but if you are going to be authorities on history you need to address all aspects of history. Bible studies are relegated to the study of theology and most theologians claim Jesus and God exist and refer to the Bible as proof — even though historical records are slim and sketchy at best."*

JR advised, *"I suggest you put the Bible on your list of reference books to read...and to be read in a manner that you can reconcile in your own mind as to whether it has historical significance that can stand up to critical scrutiny."*

JR concluded, *"I believe this has been a very productive exercise."* *"If anything, I hope it has made you think a little more....and perhaps you may want to do some further research into the claims in the Bible."*

JR added," *This discussion reminds me of something George Bernard Shaw once said:*

'Man remains what he has always been; the cruellest of all the animals, and the most elaborately fiendishly sensual.'

"Now, I don't know about you two, but I'm damn hungry — where is that waiter?" JR exclaimed.

~

References:

http://en.wikipedia.org/wiki/Pol_Pot

http://en.wikipedia.org/wiki/Mao_Zedong

http://en.wikipedia.org/wiki/Gilles_de_Rais

http://www.biography.com/people/genghis-khan-9308634#video-gallery

https://www.census.gov/population/international/data/worldpop/table_history.php

The Ten Commandments - Revisited

Exodus 34 (KJV)

And the LORD said unto Moses, *"Hew thee two tablets of stone like unto the first, and I will write upon these tablets the words that were in the first tablets which thou brakest."*

1. For thou shalt worship no other god; for the LORD, whose name is Jealous, is a jealous God.

2. Thou shalt make thee no molten gods.

3. Six days thou shalt work, but on the seventh day thou shalt rest; in plowing time and in harvest thou shalt rest.

4. Thrice in the year shall all your menchildren appear before the Lord GOD, the God of Israel.

5. The first of the first fruits of thy land thou shalt bring unto the house of the LORD thy God.

6. Thou shalt not boil a kid in his mother's milk.

7. Lest thou make a covenant with the inhabitants of the land and they go a whoring after their gods, and do sacrifice unto their gods, and one call thee and thou eat of his sacrifice.

If any of this makes sense to you than, **"God Help Us All"**. You can go to **Exodus 34** and figure what this cretin is saying. This perfect god seems to have a poor memory.

The Ten Commandments

Many religions, particularly Christians, hold up the Ten Commandments as the succinct epitome of God's highest rules to be followed. Truth be known, God has a lot more rules to be followed. But let's not quibble here. It is the 10 big ones that Christians love to quote, not necessarily follow, just quote. Some Christian groups have successfully lobbied for these commandments to be put on display in public places such as, parks, and government buildings, for example: city halls, court houses and public schools.

Just for the fun of it, let us take a look at these commandments, what they actually mean, and compare the words from a critical and a religious viewpoint. I wonder how well we have been doing in following these commandments.

1st. Commandment, Exodus 20:3 Thou shalt have no other gods before me.

Now this is straightforward. We just have one god, so why worry about any other gods…. right? Well now, this is going to be interesting. Apparently the Christian God may not be the same God even among Christians. Some Christians say there is one being known as God. Others, like the Catholic Christians, say that God is composed of 3 beings - the Trinity. Then again we find the three Abrahamic religions will disagree on which god is the true God. Muslims say it is Allah. Jews say it is Yahweh. Outside of these religions there are others, such as Hinduism, Buddhism, Sikhism, Shinto, even Scientology and Mormons, all with their own idea of God.

Here we go; right from the start we have a controversy. Which god is the real true God.........or are all of them just man-made delusions? Let us get back to the god in the Bible. What happens if you don't obey the first commandment? Here is what the Bible says:

Deuteronomy 17:1-5 *"And hath gone and served other gods, and worshipped them, either the sun, or moon, or any of the host of heavens, which I have not commanded. Then shalt thou bring forth that man or that woman, which have committed that wicked thing and <u>shalt stone them with stones, till they die"</u>.*

Deuteronomy 13:6-10 *"If thy brother, the son of thy mother, or thy son, or thy daughter, or the wife of thy bosom, or thy friend, which is of thine own soul, entice thee secretly, saying, Let us go and serve other gods, which thou hast not known, thou, nor thy fathers; Thou shalt not consent unto him, nor hearken unto him; neither shall thine eye pity him, neither shalt thou spare, neither shalt thou conceal him: <u>But thou shalt surely kill him; thine hand shall be first upon him to put him to death, and afterwards the hand of all the people. Thou shalt stone him with stones, that he die; because he hath sought to thrust thee away from the Lord thy God."</u>*

Exodus 22:20 *"He that sacrificeth unto any god, save unto the Lord only, <u>he shall be utterly destroyed"</u>.*

Mark 16:16 *"He that believeth not, <u>shall be damned"</u>.*

It is quite clear from the very first commandment there will be a good portion of the world's population that will be killed, or at the very least damned, whatever that means. I checked out various religious interpretations of "damned".

As usual we have a variety of meanings for this word. I initially thought that the passage in Mark, from the New Testament, might go a bit easier on the sinners who disobey the 1st Commandment. I was wrong. Here is what damned apparently means: It means eternal separation from the presence of God. God is the source of all life. Therefore being damned is eternal death.

Holy crackers, it doesn't mean just death, but eternal death. People actually believe this stuff!

2nd. Commandment, Exodus 20:4 Thou shalt not make unto thee any graven image, or any likeness of anything that is in heaven above, or that is on the earth beneath, or that is in the water below.

Whooaaa!!!!! This is a trick commandment. We know God likes to play tricks on people, just like he did with Abraham when he ordered him to kill his son. God was only kidding around. How many churches have graven images of God, Christ, the Virgin Mary and heavenly angels? The Vatican is chock full of graven images!!! OK, here is the trick. It's in the word "graven". What does graven mean? I looked it up. Graven means: to carve, sculpt, or engrave. That's exactly what I thought. So there is no trick. You are not supposed to carve, sculpt or engrave any image, likeness or anything that is in heaven. Oh my; somebody is in trouble.

I'm not kidding. When you try to find any kind of religious unanimity on just what this 2nd Commandment really means….good luck! Some religions do agree on what the words actually say. Most other religions take you for a dance. This one will leave your head spinning.

It's obvious to most people who can read and comprehend what they read; that most religions violate God's 2nd Commandment with total abandon.

What is the punishment for violation of the 2nd Commandment?

Deuteronomy 27:15 *"Cursed be the man that maketh any graven or molten image."*

Whew! That's not too bad, I curse all the time. To be cursed at is common place. Oops! The Bible has a different interpretation. A curse is the opposite of a blessing, whereas a blessing is a pronouncement of good fortune because one is initiated into God's plans, a curse is a pronouncement of **ill fortune because one opposes God's plans.** God may curse a person or a whole nation because of their opposition to **God's will.** It appears there are a lot of Christians that are being cursed for making graven images of those things in heaven.

3rd. Commandment, Exodus 20:7 Thou shalt not take the name of the Lord in vain

God damn it, Skeptic Cash (from Atheists on Air Podcast) you are in big trouble. Somehow, I doubt Cash is the least bit concerned. I suppose, if a good Christian hit his thumb while hammering in a nail, he could be forgiven for an outburst against God. Then there are all the folks whose prayers go unanswered, they too may also be forgiven for muttering that God never listens to them. Let us hope that there is indeed a loving, forgiving God, because here is the penalty for saying this whole God thing is a pile of B.S.

Leviticus 24:16 *"And he that blasphemeth the name of the Lord, he shall surely <u>be put to death</u>"*

Matthew 12:32 *"Whosoever speaketh against the Holy Ghost, <u>it shall not be forgiven him,</u> neither in this world, neither in the world to come".*

It looks like I am wrong again. This God is not going to be doing any forgiving.

Mark 3:29 - *"He that shall blaspheme against the Holy Ghost hath <u>never forgivness, but is in danger of eternal damnation"</u>.*

Whew! It appears, according to Mark that God left the door open just a crack, when he said <u>you are in danger</u> of eternal damnation. I am left to wonder….how many religious folks out there take the Lord's name in vain on a regular basis? Just asking?

4th. Commandment, Exodus 20:8   Remember the Sabbath day, to keep it holy.

Oh no, not this one! Working on the Sabbath. This should pretty well take care of the few Christians left who abided by the first three commandments. I know of a lot of Christians who ignore this one. Here is what one religion says about this commandment.

The text of the 4th Commandment basically says; Dedicate the day to the Lord, don't do your business or work, don't have others do your business; don't hire others to work for you. It seems quite clear to me. Now what is the punishment for working on the Sabbath?

Exodus 31:15 "Whosoever shall work in the Sabbath day, <u>he shall surely be put to death</u>".

Numbers 15:32. "And while the children of Israel were in the wilderness, they found a man that gathered sticks upon the Sabbath day…<u>And all the congregation brought him without the camp, and stoned him with stones, and he died; as the Lord commanded Moses.</u>"

I think we might not have enough stones.

5th. Commandment, Exodus 20:12   Honour thy father and thy mother.

There seems to be some confusion as to the precise meaning of this commandment. According to a Jewish interpretation, it goes something like this: *"There is no limit to the honour that is due them, and often obedience to this commandment is taxing.* [No kidding?] *The child must never shame his parents, never bring them any pain or heartache; never display anger toward them."* [Now I know you are kidding.]

Matthew 10:35-37: Jesus told his followers, *"I have come to set a man against his father, a daughter against her mother, and a daughter-in-law against her mother-in-law. And a person's enemies will be those of his own household. Anyone who loves his father or mother more than Me is not worthy of Me ..."*

When God wants one thing and your parents want something different, Jesus makes clear which master you should serve. I must say Jesus stands by his words. Read on:

Luke 2:48: Jesus sets an example. The Gospel of Luke tells us that when Jesus was 12 years old, he ran away from home. His parents, Mary and Joseph, hunted for three days before finding him in the temple.

He was meeting with a group of adult scholars who were simply mesmerized by what this young lad had to say. Luke does not spell out why Jesus chose not to tell his parents that he was going to the temple, but Luke gives us a solid clue by revealing that Mary and Joseph travelled an entire day before they even noticed their son was missing!

Luke gives us another clue by describing Mary's response to finding him again. She did not embrace her lost son with relief that he was safe, nor did she support his commitment to education. Instead she scolded him. *"Son, why have you done this to us? Your father and I have sought you anxiously."*

Luke 2:49 And did Jesus honour his mother with submission? No. He refused to apologize and even gave his mother what some would characterize as a smart-mouthed answer. *"Why did you need to search? Did you not know that I must be about my Father's business?"*

Matthew 23:9 Jesus told His followers; *"Do not call anyone on earth your father; for One is your Father, He who is in heaven* [i.e. God]."

Now we know Jesus doesn't even follow his own father's commandments. Without looking, can you take a wild guess as what is God's punishment for those who do not follow the 5th Commandment?

Exodus 21:15 *And he that smiteth his father, or his mother, shall be surely put to death.*

Exodus 21:17 *"And he that curseth his father, or his mother, shall surely be put to death".*

A religious interpretation of the above passages; maltreatment of a father and mother through striking and cursing parents were all to be placed on a par with murder, and punished in the same way. By *"smiting"* parents we are not to understand smiting to mean to kill......but any kind of maltreatment. The murder of parents is not mentioned at all, as not likely to occur and hardly conceivable. The *"cursing of parents"* is placed on a par with smiting, because it proceeds from the same disposition; and both were to be **punished with death**, because the majesty of God was violated in the persons of the parents.

That little runaway, bad-mouthing, disrespectful Jesus, who did not honour his mother and father, should have been put to death right on the spot. Of course if this was done it would have spoiled the rest of the fairy tales yet to come.

6th. Commandment, Exodus 20:13 Thou shalt not kill.

The irony of this commandment is beyond all comprehension. Once again we have a god that commands that you do as I say, not as I do. All I can say is hypocrite. The world's greatest bloodthirsty killer of all time has the audacity to tell all his little homo sapiens that they should not kill. It is obvious that most of humanity do not take this commandment seriously.

Consider for just half a second all the torturous murders committed in the name of God, by God himself, and all the religious wars in his name. Ever since Cain killed Abel people have been on a killing spree. That's what we do best. Some of the best of the best were religious leaders....all inspired by the word of God. Now this may be a silly question…but what is God's punishment for murder?

Genesis 9:6 – *"Whoso sheddeth man's blood, by man shall his blood be shed: for in the image of God made he man."*

Exodus 21:12 – *"He that smiteth a man, so that he die, shall be surely put to death."*

Leviticus 24:17 – *"And he that killeth any man shall surely be put to death."*

Matthew 5:21 – *"Ye have heard that it was said by them of old time, Thou shalt not kill; and whosoever shall kill shall be in danger of the judgment."*

Numbers 35:31 – *"Moreover ye shall take no satisfaction for the life of a murderer, which [is] guilty of death: but he shall be surely put to death."*

7th. Commandment, Exodus 20:14 Thou shalt not commit adultery.

God couldn't be more succinct. One would think that there would be very little hanky-panky going on. Well, you would be wrong.

According to statistics on adultery; Americans just love to cheat on one another. This information should not surprise anyone. Source: Associated Press, Journal of Marital and Family Therapy as of January 01, 2014.

Percent of marriages where one or both spouses admit to infidelity, either physical or emotional	41%

Percent of men who admit to committing infidelity in any relationship they've had	57%

Percentage of women who admit to committing infidelity in any relationship they've had	54%

I would expect the figures in other countries like Britain, France, Italy, Canada, etc are similar. One would also expect that religious folk, at least not very many of them, would not be breaking God's commandment. Wrong again. Below is a brief excerpt from an article that appeared in a spring, 2014 edition of the Huffington Post.

The Huffington Post recently headlined this provocative statement: **"You May Be Surprised How Many Born-Again Christians Use Ashley Madison"** (an online company that helps married people arrange affairs).

The company recently surveyed its members, and discovered that 25.1 percent are evangelical ("born-again") Christians. Catholics came in next, at 22.75 percent, followed by Protestants at 22.7 percent. The article quotes a British sociologist who explains the data*: "People who have faith often use it as an outlet for forgiveness, so they're more likely to cheat and less likely to feel guilty."*

Reverend Doctor George Campbell Morgan D.D. (December 09, 1863 – May 16, 1945) was a British evangelist, preacher and a leading Bible scholar. Here is what the good Reverend had to say about adultery.

"Unfaithfulness before marriage is as much adultery as unfaithfulness after marriage. The adulterer is the enemy of the state, and as such, after being divorced in the divorce court, should be imprisoned by the criminal courts. The man or woman upon whose guilt the marriage tie is broken, no Christian minister of any denomination has the right to remarry. It is an act of treason to the state to allow such persons to go free. They should be incarcerated in separation from the other sex to the end of their days, and then they could not wipe out the wrong they did the nation when by unchaste action they struck a blow at the family.... The prevalent notion that incompatibility of temperament is sufficient for divorce is a blow at the very throne of God.... Purity must refuse to give a moment's countenance in any form to such a doctrine of hell. The command is a simple, unqualified, irrevocable negative.... A sevenfold vice is this sin of unchaste conduct, being a sin against the Individual, the Family, the Nation, the Race, the Universe and God."

At least the good Reverend only recommended that you adulterers simply be incarcerated for the rest of your life, instead of given the death penalty. In the United States that would mean half the population would be in jail, just for having a little extra nooky. Let's see what God and his son Jesus recommends.

Leviticus 20:10 "And the man that committeth adultery with another man's wife, the adulterer and the adulteress <u>shall be put to death</u>".

Matthew 5:27-28 *"You have heard that it was said to those of old, 'You shall not commit adultery.' But I say to you that whoever looks at a woman to lust for her has already committed adultery with her in his heart."*

I would have thought Jesus would take a softer stance. Instead he condemns anyone who even thinks about getting some on the side.

8th. Commandment: Exodus 20:15 Thou shalt not steal.

There should be no confusion here. God is quite specific with regards to punishment.

Exodus 22:1-4 Property Rights *"If a man steals an ox or a sheep and slaughters it or sells it, he shall pay five oxen for the ox and four sheep for the sheep. If the thief is caught while breaking in and is struck so that he dies, there will be no bloodguiltiness on his account. But if the sun has risen on him, there will be bloodguiltiness on his account. He shall surely make restitution; if he owns nothing, then he shall be sold for his theft. If what he stole is actually found alive in his possession, whether an ox or a donkey or a sheep, he shall pay double."*

It sure is nice to know what happens if my donkey is stolen. I can't find a specific passage that says you will be killed if you steal. As things stand, if you are going to break any of the commandments, this one looks like the safest one to break.

However, be careful, if you kidnap someone, this kind of theft will result in......you guessed it, **death.**

Exodus 21:16 *"And he that stealet a man, and selleth him, or if he be found in his hand, he shall surely be <u>put to death.</u>"*

9th. Commandment, Exodus 20:16   Thou shalt not bear false witness against thy neighbour.

Quite simply, we are commanded to speak the truth in all things, but especially in what concerns the good name and honour of others. There is not much more to be said about this commandment, for most people it is straightforward.

Exodus 23:1-2 *"You shall not spread a false report. You shall not join hands with a wicked man to be a malicious witness. You shall not fall in with the many to do evil, nor shall you bear witness in a lawsuit, siding with the many, so as to pervert justice, nor shall you be partial to a poor man in his lawsuit."*

Ephesians 4:25 *"Wherefore, put away lying and speak truth each one with his XXXneighbour, because we are members of one another."*

Proverbs 12:22 *"Lying lips are an abomination to the Lord."*

Ecclesiasticus 7:13 *"Devise not a lie against thy brother, neither do the like against thy friend."*

I could not find a specific passage in the Bible that states the punishment for lying. Many theologians apparently advise that the punishment is the same as breaking any of the other commandments....**that is death.**

10th. Commandment "You shall not covet"

Here is the complete commandment: *"You shall not covet your neighbour's house; you shall not covet your neighbour's wife, nor his male servant, nor his female servant, nor his ox, nor his donkey, nor anything that is your neighbour's."*

This simply means stop trying to keep up with the Joneses. In other words, you are not supposed to desire or want what others have. In other words, God is against the American way of life. Maybe that's not exactly what God meant.

It is more like; you cannot even think about having anything of your neighbours. I don't need to worry about this one as my neighbour's house is a dive, his wife is a bitch, he doesn't have any servants or an ox. He does have a big ass however, but most of the time he is sitting on it while guzzling beer. (Just kidding folks, I have nice neighbours)

So there it is the so-called 10 big ones. You really must ask yourself if all these God believers actually follow these commands. We know they don't. If you find it difficult to follow these so-called commandments of God you may want to consider a different set of commandments. I'd rather call them ideals. Ideals are principles, standards, morals and ethics. They are ideas of something that strives toward perfection. Ideals could also be described as goals and behaviour that one hopes to attain.

And don't worry if you can't live up to them. No one will sentence you to death.

~

Richard Dawkins' Ten Commandments

1. Do not do to others what you would not want them to do to you.

2. In all things, strive to cause no harm.

3. Treat your fellow human beings, your fellow living things, and the world in general with love, honesty, faithfulness and respect.

4. Do not overlook evil or shrink from administering justice, but always be ready to forgive wrongdoing freely admitted and honestly regretted.

5. Live life with a sense of joy and wonder.

6. Always seek to be learning something new.

7. Test all things; always check your ideas against the facts, and be ready to discard even a cherished belief if it does not conform to them.

8. Never seek to censor or cut yourself off from dissent; always respect the right of others to disagree with you.

9. Form independent opinions on the basis of your own reason and experience; do not allow yourself to be led blindly by others.

10. Question everything.

(Source: thetumblratheist)

My 10 Beliefs

1. I BELIEVE when humanity makes the paradigm shift from individual well-being to global well-being; the world will see the dawn of a new renaissance.

Why: Globalization has demonstrated the world's people have become increasingly dependent on each other. We must rethink the selfish notion of **my** well-being to **our** well-being; otherwise, eventually everyone's well-being is in jeopardy.

2. I BELIEVE humanity's greatest failure is the use of war to settle disputes. Humanity's greatest success is the indomitable spirit of renewal.

Why: Killing one another must surely be accepted, by any measuring stick, as wrong. Yet we continue the killing spree in spite of our internal drive for renewal. The challenge we face is to rethink why we continue to kill; and seek new solutions to this, the greatest threat to humanity.

3. I BELIEVE when generosity, conservation, liberty, humility, and compassion is embraced, human evolution will reach a defining moment in history.

Why: A pessimist might state that greed, over-consumption, oppression, egoism, and revenge dominate our world. Whatever the truth, I believe we must continually think and rethink the dominant principles that best serve humanity.

4. I BELIEVE it is abhorrent to disguise the crimes against humanity in the name of any deity, superstition or dogma.

Why: Religious crimes, Nazi crimes, North Korean crimes, etc; the killings, the genocides, the tortures, all committed against humanity in the name of some belief as being acceptable is the antithesis of humanism.

5. I BELIEVE the human species is not separate and apart from all of nature's creations; our existence is tied to theirs.

Why: We need to rethink how our human activities, technology and appetite for growth, affects our environment and all animal and plant life that sustains the human race. We are as much dependent on sustaining; for example the lives of the honey bee, as the honey bee sustains us.

6. I BELIEVE to not challenge authority and accept the motto: *"to get along, go along"* will demonstrate how quickly humanity can descend into barbarism.

Why: Freedom, in all its forms, is only free when authority can meet the challenges of critical questioning. To not question authority is to surrender your freedom.

7. I BELIEVE ideas are born through freedom of thought; stagnation is born through dogma, and advancement through inquiry.

Why: When I think of how religious dogma has held back human progress, not only in physics, but also in our humanistic view of the world, I submit that freedom of thought is vital to human progress.

8. I BELIEVE superstition creates fear; knowledge defeats fear; society is the arbiter over which one is their compass.

Why: Among the great motivators in life are fear, reward, love, faith, hope and knowledge. Pick your motivator. I pick knowledge.

9. I BELIEVE every drop of rain that falls can enrich life; and every word so spoken can advance or retard humanity.

Why: Too many people think their words don't count. All words count, whether they come from a parent, a teacher, a pastor or a homeless vagabond. It is vital for atheists to raise their voices on behalf of humanity.

10. I BELIEVE if you own the narrative; you control the world.

Why: Whatever the word, which is believed by the people as being the truth, humanity seems hard-wired to follow. The narrative must be humanism.

The above ten beliefs are my thoughts, in my own words. I would like to think of them as original, but I know most, if not all have been expressed by others throughout the ages. On the Ten Commandments, and the other information in this section I received some help from the following websites:

~

http://www.evilbible.com/ten_commandments.htm   (more specific: The Church of Theists Suck)

http://atheism.about.com/od/bibledictionaryonline/p/curses cursing.htm

http://www.answerbag.com/q_view/2493935

http://www.divinerevelations.info/documents/misc/keep_sa
bbath_holy/

http://www.proyouthpages.com/5thcommandment.html

http://www.hebrew4christians.com/Scripture/Torah/Ten_C
mds/Fifth_Cmd/fifth_cmd.html

http://www.bibletools.org/index.cfm/fuseaction/Topical.sho
w/RTD/cgg/ID/536/Fifth-Commandment.htm

http://www.positiveatheism.org/hist/lewis/lewten71.htm

http://www.statisticbrain.com/infidelity-statistics/

http://www.denisonforum.org/cultural-commentary/1065-
are-born-again-christians-more-likely-to-commit-adultery

http://www.catholicity.com/baltimore-
catechism/lesson20.html

http://www.patheos.com/blogs/christiancrier/2014/05/26/w
hat-does-covet-mean-bible-definition-of-covet-or-coveting/

http://thetumblratheist.tumblr.com/post/6943999339/richar
d-dawkins-ten-commandments

Atrocities in the Name of God

"I have wiped out many nations, devastating their fortress walls and towers. Their cities are now deserted; their streets are in silent ruin. There are no survivors to even tell what happened. I thought, 'Surely they will have reverence for me now! Surely they will listen to my warnings, so I won't need to strike again.' But no; however much I punish them, they continue their evil practices from dawn till dusk and dusk till dawn." So now the LORD says: "Be patient; the time is coming soon when I will stand up and accuse these evil nations. For it is my decision to gather together the kingdoms of the earth and pour out my fiercest anger and fury on them. All the earth will be devoured by the fire of my jealousy. "On that day I will purify the lips of all people, so that everyone will be able to worship the LORD together. My scattered people who live beyond the rivers of Ethiopia will come to present their offerings." **- (Zephaniah 3:6-10 NLT)**

Atrocities in the Name of God

Some deluded people have this urge to kill in the name of God or religion. There are many accounts of people killing in the name of religion. Some of these killings are so embedded in the public's consciousness that there is no need to elabourate upon them. The Islamic extremist terrorists attack on the world Trade Centre in New York City, commonly referred to as 9-11, will remain as a record of history. This attack, on American soil, was a turning point for many believers. It set them on the path to atheism.

In this section, I attempt to bring the discussion back to some of the most horrific of crimes committed in the name of religion. Some of these events are in the Bible; as unbelievable as they are. Other events are fading from public memory. I suspect that many who read this book may never have heard of some of these atrocities. However monstrous these events were, and remembering them may cause too much pain; it would be a mistake to forget them.

Many people do not wish to be told or reminded of such atrocities. They go along their merry life as if all is lollipops and roses. I am not suggesting we should be reliving these terrible events every minute of our existence. Life is indeed too short. We must live life to the fullest and spread happiness and joy whenever we can. Somehow we must strike a balance. We must support each other, enjoy the good times, but not be blinkered to the evils of the past or the evils around us. One of those evils is religion.

A woman friend of mine simply refuses to watch movies that focus on the mistreatment, torture and killing of people. She will not watch movies such *as 'Schindler's List'*, *'Sophie's Choice'* or *'Life is Beautiful'*.

She finds these movies just too painful to watch. This woman is religious. Much to my surprise, she did go to see the movie, *'Passion of the Christ'*; because her Catholic priest suggested she do so. She could not watch most of the movie as it was too upsetting. Actually, half the movie was just scenes of torture. She came away from the movie theatre visibly shaking, with tears flowing.

As I write this piece, two Canadian soldiers were viciously mowed down within a matter of a two day time span. One of the killers used his car to run over a soldier in a parking lot. The other was shot in cold blood just outside Canada's parliament buildings, while on duty as a guard, at Canada's memorial of the Unknown Soldier. Both soldiers were killed by religious, homicidal maniacs in broad daylight. Both soldiers were killed not in a foreign land during open warfare but instead they were slaughtered in two separate unrelated incidents while going about their daily life. Canadians are a peace-loving, caring society. Canadians welcome people from all over the world to share their life and enjoy each others culture in a spirit of multi-cultural friendship. And yet, both killers were home grown terrorists.

As I edit this book, more madness took place in France. Satirical cartoons in the publication, "Charlie Hebdo" were the insane justification for the murder of 12 people; mostly cartoonists and journalists. These delusional fanatics have a sick infatuation with Islamic terrorist groups that call for a total Islamic state. Such a state would outlaw all religions, except their perverted version of Islam.

Sadly, these two Canadian soldiers will soon be forgotten, just like the many others who have been killed in the name of one religion or another. Perhaps the events in France may cause the world to wake up; but I doubt it.

We continue to lurch from one massacre to the next. We always hear the same sanctimonious comments from world leaders and religious heads saying things like; *"The victims and their families are in our prayers."*

Sam Harris has contributed a great amount of thought-provoking material on this subject. He has raised the level of discussion, and issued chilling warnings concerning the dangers of religious dogmas. His words cuts through the madness of religious teachings like a laser beam.

"We have a choice. We have two options as human beings. We have a choice between conversation and war. That's it. Conversation or violence. And faith is a conversation stopper." — Sam Harris; American author, philosopher, and neuroscientist

Historical Atrocities Fading
from the Public Memory

September Dawn is a feature film starring John Voight, Terrance Stamp and Trent Ford. It apparently did not do well at the box office. The movie is based upon the true story of the **Mountain Meadows Massacre** – the brutal murder of 120 men, women and children on September 11, 1857. It is one of those atrocities about which little are known. Some still question whether the attack was carried out by local Indians or by a sect of the Mormon Church.

There was a series of attacks on a wagon train heading to California through southern Utah. The mass slaughter of the emigrant party, mostly from Arkansas, encountered the Mormon's who feigned friendship. All the while the Mormon's conspired with some local Indians, known as the Paiute, to massacre the travellers.

Under the leadership of those in the local military, church and government organizations, Isaac C. Haight and John D. Lee, conspired. Lee lead militiamen, disguised as Indians, along with a contingent of Paiute tribesmen, in an attack. The travellers fought back, and a siege ensued. Intending to leave no witnesses of the Mormon complicity in the siege, the militiamen tricked the travellers to surrender and give up their weapons. After which, they promised, all would be safely escorted out of the county.

This was a trap to leave the travellers defenceless. Amazingly, the travellers agreed to separate the men, women and children. The brutal cold-blooded massacre was horrific. Everyone was killed except for seventeen children, who at the time were too young to speak. An investigation of the massacre was ordered and held under the leadership of U.S. Army Major James H. Carleton. In 1859 Carleton visited the site of the massacre. Carleton issued a scathing report to the United States Congress, blaming local and senior church leaders for the massacre. Investigations were interrupted by the American Civil War, and it wasn't until 1874 that nine indictments were ordered. Of the men indicted, only John D. Lee was tried in a court of law. After two trials, Lee was finally convicted and executed near the massacre site.

The causes and circumstances of the Mountain Meadows Massacre remain contested and highly controversial. Although there is no evidence that Brigham Young ordered or condoned the massacre, the involvement of various church officials, in both the murders and concealing evidence in their aftermath, is still questioned. Moreover, while by all accounts, Native American Paiutes were present, historical reports of their numbers and the details of their participation are contradictory.

While some of the survivors were very young, and their memories of events non-conclusive, the ancestors of those massacred, to this day, claim justice was never done and much was covered-up. A website in their memory may be found at: http://1857massacre.com/index.htm

Dena Schlosser (born 1969) is a Plano, Texas woman who, on November 22, 2004, amputated the arms of her eleven-month-old daughter, Margaret, with a knife. Plano police responded to a 9-1-1 call made by concerned workers at a local day care center who had spoken to Schlosser earlier that day. The 9-1-1 operator testified that Schlosser confessed to her and that the gospel song, *"He Touched Me"* played in the background. When police arrived, they saw Schlosser covered in blood and calmly sitting holding the knife singing Christian hymns.

Schlosser had been investigated earlier that year by the Texas Child Protective Services, who had decided she did not pose a risk to her children. The baby died the following day; her other two daughters were not harmed.

Psychiatrist David Self testified that Schlosser told him that she had interpreted a television news story about a boy being mauled by a lion as a sign of the coming apocalypse, and that she had heard God commanding her to remove her baby's arm and then her own. The attack was later described as *"religious frenzy"*. Dr. Self determined that Dena Schlosser suffered from postpartum psychosis.

She was found not guilty by reason of insanity, and was committed to the North Texas State Hospital and ordered to stay there until she was deemed to no longer be a threat to herself or others.

Coincidentally, she was a roommate of Andrea Yates; the Houston, Texas woman who had drowned her five children in a bathtub, which she says was done to protect them from Satan.

John Schlosser, Dena Schlosser's husband, later filed for divorce. As part of the divorce settlement, Dena Schlosser was prohibited from having any contact with either her ex-husband or her daughters again.

On November 6, 2008, it was announced that Dena Schlosser would shortly be released into outpatient care. The order required her to see a psychiatrist once a week, take medication, be on physician-approved birth control, and not have any unsupervised contact with children.

See: http://murderpedia.org/female.S/s/schlosser-dena.htm
Juan Ignacio Blanco crime reporter & criminalist

Ministry of Terror

The Jonestown Cult Massacre by Elissa Haney (written in the late 1990's)

Two decades ago an unusual series of events led to the deaths of more than 900 people in the middle of a South American jungle. Though dubbed a "massacre," what transpired at Jonestown on November 18, 1978, was to some extent done willingly, making the mass suicide all the more disturbing.

The Jonestown cult (officially named the "People's Temple") was founded in 1955 by Indianapolis preacher James Warren Jones. Jones, who had no formal theological training, based his liberal ministry on a combination of religious and socialist philosophies.

A New, Isolated Community

After relocating to California in 1965, the church continued to grow in membership and began advocating their left-wing political ideals more actively. With an I.R.S. investigation and a great deal of negative press mounting against the radical church, Jones urged his congregation to join him in a new, isolated community where they could escape American capitalism—and criticism—and practice a more communal way of life.

In 1977, Jones and many of his followers relocated to Jonestown, on a tract of land the People's Temple had purchased and begun to develop three years earlier.

Relatives of cult members soon grew concerned and requested that the U.S. government rescue what they believed to be brainwashed victims living in concentration camp-like conditions under Jones's power.

The Visit of Congressman Ryan

In November 1978, California Congressman Leo Ryan arrived in Guyana to survey Jonestown and interview its inhabitants. After reportedly having his life threatened by a Temple member during the first day of his visit, Ryan decided to cut his trip short and return to the U.S. with some Jonestown residents who wished to leave. As they boarded their plane, a group of Jones's guards opened fire on them, killing Ryan and four others.

Some members of Ryan's party escaped, however. Upon learning this, Jones told his followers that Ryan's murder would make it impossible for their commune to continue functioning.

Rather than return to the United States, the People's Temple would preserve their church by making the ultimate sacrifice: their own lives. Jones's 912 followers were given a deadly concoction of purple Kool-Aid mixed with cyanide, sedatives, and tranquilizers. Jones apparently shot himself in the head.

Source: The Jonestown Massacre | Infoplease.com http://www.infoplease.com/spot/jonestown1.html#ixzz3Gh pF4xUz

Hidden No Longer: Genocide in Canada, Past and Present - by Kevin D. Annett, M.A., M.Div.

I could never do justice to what Kevin Annett has written, so I won't try. I will simply provide you with this man's background, the preamble to his book, and the location where you may read this book on-line, at **no cost**. I really shouldn't say at **no cost**. There is a cost.

My heart breaks and I can't hold back my tears when reading such atrocities. It is a tough read; and I expect many will not be able to finish reading his book. If you have one little speck of humanity in your bones, you cannot help but suffer an emotional cost. It will take its toll and leave you shivering.

The book is full of original documents, letters and pictures. If you can bear up to the challenge, then do so. If you can't, it is not necessary to read the entire book. If you can brace yourself for 20 minutes, then perhaps a reading from pages 68 to 88 will be enough to tell part of this horrible story.

When it comes to the mistreatment of children I have a difficult time writing anything. It leaves me an emotional wreck. I admit I am not strong enough to buck-up. I seethe with anger, and it takes every bit of courage to restrain myself so that I do not lash out in an uncontrollable rage.

I therefore must rely on others to tell the stories of child abuse and leave it for readers to draw their own conclusions.

Background of Kevin Annett

Kevin Daniel Annett is a community minister, educator, author and award-winning documentary film maker who lives and works among indigenous and low income people in Vancouver, Canada. He is the host of several public affairs radio programs, and is a consultant to survivors of church torture around the world. Kevin holds Masters Degrees in Political Science and Theology from the University of British Columbia and the Vancouver School of Theology.

A former minister in the United Church of Canada, Kevin was fired without cause and expelled from the church without due process in 1997 after he challenged church officers with evidence of murders and other crimes committed by them in their Indian residential schools. Kevin was adopted into the Anishinabe (Ojibway) Nation in Winnipeg in 2004 and given the name Eagle Strong Voice by Chief Louis Daniels (Whispering Wind) in recognition for "his selfless and courageous stand for indigenous people".

Founder of the first non-governmental Truth Commission into crimes of genocide by church and state in Canada, in 2000, Kevin recently united survivors of church terror in seven nations to form The International Tribunal into Crimes of Church and State. He is a member of the Council of Elders of the Party for the Republic of Kanata. His documentary film UNREPENTANT has won numerous international awards and is broadcast regularly around the world.

Preamble to: Hidden No Longer: Genocide in Canada, Past and Present

If James Joyce is right, and history is a nightmare from which we are trying to awaken, then it is also true that victory belongs to those who can remember. Twenty years ago, soon after my ordination as a clergyman in the United Church of Canada, I first began to hear stories of what my church had done to innocent children in its Indian residential schools. Like most people, I didn't believe the accounts of murder and torture I was hearing. And if I had have kept my ears and heart closed to these tales, I would have been spared an enormous personal loss and liberation. But fate, and choice, forced me not only to listen, but give voice and a platform to hundreds, and then thousands of indigenous men and women whose stories you will read in these pages. And as a result, the face of Canada has been changed forever. But the ones you won't hear from are the more than 50,000 children who died from beatings, starvation, rape and torture, or being deliberately exposed to tuberculosis and left to cough their lives away in squalor and terror: all at the hands of Christian men and women who have never been prosecuted for their crimes. These murdered children lie in nearly-forgotten graves across Canada, or their ashes are scattered on sea and land after they were incinerated in residential school furnaces, to hide the crime that killed them. But they have not vanished, and their day is coming, thanks in part to the work and campaigns associated with this book.

This book is dedicated to the more than 50,000 children who died in "Indian residential schools" operated jointly by the government of Canada and the Roman Catholic, Anglican and United Church of Canada – and to those who continue to suffer and die from the consequences of these crimes.

For more information about the author or this work's sponsoring organizations, or to order copies, please see these sites:
www.hiddenfromhistory.org http://canadiangenocide.native web.org

Or contact the author at: hiddenfromhistory1@yahoo.ca

ph: 250-591-4573 (Canada)

Published on Occupied Territory of the Squamish Indigenous Nation September, 2010

Note: It would appear that changes have been made to this website and the author's book is not available to read free of charge, but may be purchased. However the chilling report of this genocide can be viewed at this revised website. It is truly unbelievable.

Atrocities in the Bible

Children & Women

Psalms 137: 8-9: *"O daughter of Babylon, who art to be destroyed; happy shall he be, that rewardeth thee as thou hast served us. Happy shall he be, that taketh and dasheth thy little ones against the stones."*

King David, who Jews praise as one of their great leaders, is said to be the author of the Psalms. This is the same young David who slew Goliath and took delight in cutting off the giant's head. You may have heard of the House of David, well this is the same David who is glorified. This David fellow carried-out many of God's killing orders and he did so with gusto. He was one of God's greatest killing machines.

So what is this thing about smashing the children of Babylon against the stones? Is it all about revenge? In fact most of God's and David's killings are about revenge. Speak about contradictions; here is what I found in **Leviticus 19:18** - *"Thou shalt not avenge, nor bear any grudge against the children of thy people, but thou shalt love thy neighbour as thyself: I am the LORD."* OK, everyone; give your head a shake.

Now here we have God or King David saying to take the children of Babylon, smash them against the stones …and be happy. What kind of sick bastard would be happy about committing such an atrocious act of inhumanity? Christians tie themselves in knots over this Bible passage. The rest of us place our face into the palms of our hands in total disbelief.

I can't count the number of times I have recited in church the 23 Psalm. You know the one; it starts: *"The Lord is my shepherd…"*, but nary a mention ever, anytime, not once of Psalm 137. It makes one wonder why?

Warning! Warning! Warning!
It gets pretty damn disgusting!!!!

Deuteronomy 28: 53-57 New International Version (NIV)

53*: "Because of the suffering your enemy will inflict on you during the siege, you will eat the fruit of the womb, the flesh of the sons and daughters the LORD your God has given you."*

54: *"Even the most gentle and sensitive man among you will have no compassion on his own brother or the wife he loves or his surviving children,"*

55: *"and he will not give to one of them any of the flesh of his children that he is eating. It will be all he has left because of the suffering your enemy will inflict on you during the siege of all your cities."*

56: *"The most gentle and sensitive woman among you— so sensitive and gentle that she would not venture to touch the ground with the sole of her foot—will begrudge the husband she loves and her own son or daughter;"*

57: *"the afterbirth from her womb and the children she bears. For in her dire need she intends to eat them secretly because of the suffering your enemy will inflict on you during the siege of your cities."*

Are you ready to vomit? Pardon my language…but what the fuck is going on here? Is this disgusting, repulsive, sickening and nauseating behaviour the orders from the god that Christians pray to? Is this the so-called loving god where Christians get their morality? If this is what any religious person claim is moral, then I don't want any part of it. Get a life!

Here is what Study Light has to say. Since March 22, 2001, StudyLight.org has been providing Bible resources to the Christian Internet community. Starting with a handful of Bibles and reference tools, the site has grown to be the leader in online resources.

Verse 53

.And thou shalt eat the fruit of thine own body. This is one of those portents which was mentioned a little while ago; for it is an act of ferocity detestable and more than tragic, that fathers and mothers should eat their own offspring, so great love of which is naturally implanted in every heart, that parents often forget themselves in their anxiety for their children; and many have not hesitated to die to insure their safety. Nay, when the brute animals so carefully cherish their young, what can be more disgusting or abominable than that men should cease to care for their own blood? But this is the most monstrous of all atrocities, when fathers and mothers devour the offspring which they have procreated, and yet this threat by no means failed of its fulfillment, as we have elsewhere seen. We ought then to be the more alarmed when we see that God thus terribly punished the sins of those whom He had deigned to choose for His own.

Still, it was not without very just cause that this wrath was so greatly kindled against the Jews who had left no kind of iniquity undone, so that their wickedness was altogether intolerable. **Never, then, must it be forgotten that those of the household of the Church to whom God's truth is revealed, are on that account the less excusable, because they knowingly and wilfully provoke His wrath, whilst their continued perseverance in sin is altogether unworthy of pardon.**

The monstrous brutality of the act is heightened, when He says that men, in other respects tender and accustomed to delicacies, should be so savage through hunger that they shall refuse to give a share of this horrible food to their wives and surviving children; as also Jeremiah expressly says, the pitiful women shall be so maddened by hunger as to cook their own children. (Lamentations 4:10.) What follows as to the after-birth is still more horrible, for thus they call the membrane by which the foetus is covered in the womb, with all its excrements. That they should dress for food a filthy skin, the very look of which is disgusting, plainly demonstrates the awfulness of God's vengeance.

Holy shit, I was never told this in church. Since Lamentations is referenced, let us check this one a little further.

Lamentations 4: 8-11 *"Their appearance is blacker than soot, They are not recognized in the streets; Their skin is shriveled on their bones, It is withered, it has become like wood. Better are those slain with the sword Than those slain with hunger; For they pine away, being stricken For lack of the fruits of the field. The hands of compassionate women Boiled their own children; They became food for them Because of the destruction of the daughter of my people. The LORD has accomplished His wrath..."*

And they call this the **'Good Book'**? For over 50 years I had no idea such disgusting filth existed in the pages of the Bible. I really have difficulty understanding how any of this was at all possible. I keep reminding myself that all of this is made-up stories by ignorant men who could only be described as primitive, uncivilized barbarians. And yet Christians continue to praise this angry God.

Need I remind you what the religious apologists say? Do you remember? Let me remind you.

"Never, then, must it be forgotten that those of the household of the Church to whom God's truth is revealed, are on that account the less excusable, because they knowingly and wilfully provoke His wrath, whilst their continued perseverance in sin is altogether unworthy of pardon."

All you Christians, who know God's truth, therefore have no excuse. Do any of you Christians work on the Sabbath? Have any of you had an extramarital affair? Have any of you ever said; "God damn it!" Well, you sinners are unworthy of being pardoned. Be warned; the wrath of God may come down upon you. Think I'm kidding? Let's take a look at what the Lord told Moses.

Penalty for Violating the Sabbath

Numbers 15: 32-36 New King James Version (NKJV)
"Now while the children of Israel were in the wilderness, they found a man gathering sticks on the Sabbath day. And those who found him gathering sticks brought him to Moses and Aaron, and to all the congregation. They put him under guard, because it had not been explained what should be done to him."

"Then the LORD said to Moses, "The man must surely be put to death; all the congregation shall stone him with stones outside the camp." So, as the LORD commanded Moses, all the congregation brought him outside the camp and stoned him with stones, and he died."

All of this is pretty sick stuff. And I will never know why certain thoughts pop into my head. When I read this nonsense from the Bible my emotions vacillate between anger, incredulity and laughter. Honestly, one must be delusional if they take this seriously.

This is insane punishment ordered by this Christian God who is psychotic. There are times when I don't know if to laugh or cry.

There was a children's song that all my friends used to sing sometimes at church outings. Why this song sprung to mind I don't know. In the last stanza I changed a couple of the words. The song goes like this:

This old man he played six,
He played knick knack on his sticks;
With a knick knack paddy whack,
Give the dog a bone,
This old man; oh he got stoned.

If you had told me 20 years ago that there are approximately 100 more atrocities in the Bible, just like the ones above, I would have said you are a liar.

Actually, there are so many atrocities and killings they would fill a book. In fact, Steve Wells has written a book called **'Drunk with Blood – God's Killings in the Bible'**.

I don't know exactly how many times God went on a killing rampage, I just got too tired of counting. At least Steve Wells has given us a pretty good count. All told, Mr. Wells estimates that this loving god has been responsible for at least 25,000,000 deaths. Now this twenty-five million was at a time when the world had a population of only a few million, not 7 billion, as it is today. Just think about the carnage God could create today if he really set his killing machine loose.

Now this is going to sound repetitious. Remember what I said in the Introduction about writing something only to find someone else had written similar thoughts. Mr. Wells and I share an opinion. Here is an excerpt from what he has to say.

"Bible believers, on the other hand, are less proud of god's killings. Oh, they like a few of them – Noah's flood, Sodom and Gomorrah, Jericho- those that can be made (with considerable dishonesty) into cute children's stories. But the rest are either completely ignored or completely unknown to believers."

"I believe that most believers would stop believing in the Bible if they knew what was in it. And this is particularly true of God's killings. All of the stories are absurd from a historical standpoint; they could not have happened the way they are told in the Bible.

But what is even more damning is their unspeakable cruelty and obvious immorality. If the killings described in this book actually happened, then the God of the Bible is not the kind of god that believers pretend him to be." - Steve Wells

Moses' Mass Murder

Numbers 31:16-18 *"Behold, these caused the children of Israel, through the counsel of Balaam, to commit trespass against the LORD in the matter of Peor, and there was a plague among the congregation of the LORD. Now therefore kill every male among the little ones, and kill every woman that hath known man by lying with him. But all the women children, that have not known a man by lying with him, keep alive for yourselves."*

Moses commands the murder of approximately 100,000 young males and, roughly, 68,000 helpless women. This is just one more massacre ordered by this loving God. First, let us have a brief history lesson here. Just who are these people? According to Genesis; the Midianites were the descendants of Midan, who was a son of Abraham. Yes, that's right, a son of Abraham. They were Israelites. They were all Israelites. And all they ever did was kill each other, usually upon the command of God. You see God kept getting pissed-off with these different groups or tribes of Jews. All through the Jewish history God just can't seem to get these people to behave, no matter how many he killed, tortured, or how many plagues he set upon them. They still disobey. Since the time of Adam and Eve, all through the time of Noah, Abraham, Isaac, Jacob, Joseph, and Moses; they just could not get the message straight. So God's blood lust continued with Joshua, David and a host of others.

This time it was the Midianites. What was their crime? First, you must remember they are part of the Israelite family of tribes, and at one time were all quite friendly. However, like so many of the Israelites, they strayed like little lost lambs. Apparently, they didn't understand the message from God that was given through Moses.

They formed an association with the Moabites; another group of outcasts. Together, they were thought to have worshipped a multitude of gods, including Baal-peor and the Queen of Heaven, Austerity. The Midianites may have also worshiped Yahweh, the other name of the God of Moses' burning bush. It just so happens that the burning bush was at the far end of the Midian's wilderness. However, it remains uncertain which deities the Midianites actually worshiped.

In any case, the point is not up for discussion. Remember God's first commandment. If you worship any other god you are dead meat. How could they possibly forget the very first commandment? Boy, these people are stupid. But do stupid people deserve to be slaughtered with such abandon?

Just for a moment, consider the optics of this massacre. Consider if these were women and children of your own family; your wife, daughter, sons, uncles, cousins, etc. How would you feel if a man, claiming to speak for God, sent men into your house and hacked to pieces the women and children? How would you react if these men spotted a female child, and dragged her off to do as they pleased with her? When you consider the present day Islamic extremists like ISIS or if you prefer ISIL (either way it means Islamic State) not much have changed.

"Sticks and stones may break my bones; but names will never hurt me."

Some may have heard this little chant before: Don't believe it, especially if you offend God or one of his prophets. You see, there was this fellow named Elisha. He was rather thin-skinned and a bit of a reactionary, just like his ill-tempered invisible friend.

When God and Elisha conspire together you had better hold your tongue. Let us see what happens when a couple of mocking youngsters mouth-off.

Elisha Is Jeered - 2 Kings 2:23-24 New International Version (NIV) *"From there Elisha went up to Bethel. As he was walking along the road, some boys came out of the town and jeered at him.* "Get out of here, baldy!" *they said.* "Get out of here, baldy!" *He turned around, looked at them and called down a curse on them in the name of the LORD. Then two bears came out of the woods and mauled forty-two of the boys."*

You really must imagine this scene being acted out. Old Baldy, the Prophet, is walking through town. A group of kids taunt him. Now don't forget Elisha's all knowing, all powerful buddy is up there in the sky. Even in some of the most primitive societies a heavenly whack across the kids' heads might serve the purpose. Then maybe a thundering crack of lightning out of the blue, at the feet of the kids, should set them straight. That would surely make the kids scatter and help them think twice the next time they decide to mouth-off. Unfortunately, our loving God just doesn't operate in this fashion. This over-the-top megalomaniac just loves his murderous ways. He falls back on his blood and guts option.

Now try to picture this; two bears come out of the woods and rip the heads, arms and legs off of 42 kids. I'm not sure what today's punishment would be for kids calling a priest 'baldy', but having them mauled by bears seems a tad extreme. Another thing seems most curious; these bears must have moved at supernatural speed. Wouldn't you think if there were 42 kids that they would run like hell in every direction to get away? None of this makes any sense, unless of course you are deluded by religion.

If you are interesting in reading a very long debate among bloggers you can go to this site:
http://dwindlinginunbelief.blogspot.ca/2009/10/bad-news-bears-guest-post-from-brucker.html

In October 2009, Steve Wells invited a blogger, known as Brucker to explore this Bible passage with him. Brucker has an active blog and is a Christian apologist. Their exchange on this topic makes for interesting reading. I've inserted a very brief excerpt from their extensive exchange of viewpoints.

Steve Wells: *"So it is right to kill children in a cruel way as long as it's for a good purpose, like discouraging people from insulting a prophet."*

Brucker: *"You know, one of the big reasons I've never been worried about your list of God's killings is that from a theological perspective, it's not really at all troubling that God kills people. Everyone dies eventually, and in the face of eternity, you're going to spend far more time in the afterlife than here on earth anyway. (On a side note, this theological stance informs my view that while abortion is a bad thing, I don't think it's because it hurts the embryo; but that's another matter I don't want to get into.)"*

"Cruelty is the issue that remains to be addressed, though. Getting mauled by bears can't be pleasant. Unfortunately, I don't have a good answer for this, other than to say that while I think these are kids, I do think they were old enough to be responsible for their own actions to some extent. And of course as a Christian, I have to assume God knows what He's doing. – "

Steve Wells: *"So God can kill people for any reason any way he likes and it doesn't bother you at all, because you look at it from "a theological perspective." He can send bears to rip apart children for saying "go away, baldy", burn people to death for complaining, bury them alive for pretty much no reason at all."*

This back and forth went on for some time. Then a fellow; Dave B. had his say.

Dave B: *"Hi Steve, Brucker, et al. I participated in Steve's original 2 Kings 2:23 posting, and just now discovered this new thread. Good stuff. This story was a catalyst that began my journey away from Christianity nearly 10 years ago I got a knot in my chest when I was reading this story to my then small children from one of the Bible story books for children."*

"Not much to add here, but Brucker made a statement that brought that all back. Brucker said," "...from a theological perspective, it's not really at all troubling that God kills people."

"A fascinating statement that pretty much sums up (to me anyway) why I now detest religion. In worshipping a murdering tyrant, Brucker, you have simply lost your humanity."

"The non-believers here (and on every religious blog I participate in) are the ones expressing compassion for their fellow human beings. Christians, on the other hand, spend considerable time with cognitive dissonance and must continuously justify in their minds why a loving omniscient omnipotent creator would knowingly create a world where he would murder his own creation, including his own son. It is sick."

Should you have a problem finding the entire thread to this interesting discussion try Google:

'The Bad-News Bears: A guest post from Brucker'

According to Jesus
The Sermon on the Mount

[The audience members at the back of the crowd are having trouble hearing the Sermon on the Mount.]

Man: *"I think it was;"* *["Blessed are the cheese makers"!]*

Gregory's wife: *"What's so special about the cheese makers?"*

Gregory: *"Well, obviously it's not meant to be taken literally. It refers to any manufacturer of dairy products."*

-Dialogue from the movie: Life of Brian

"There is a passage on the Sermon on the Mount that is so radical that it's doubtful that our Defence Department would survive its application."

- attributed to Barack Obama, President of the United States

According to Jesus

According to the Bible, Jesus made some interesting statements, claims, predictions, and issued confusing reprimands. Here are some of his, shall I say, more charming of the lot. A treasure trove of his edicts can be found in his famous Sermon on the Mount.

The Sermon on the Mount – Matthew 5-7

When first I was told about Jesus and his famous sermon, I thought how wonderful a message. I have a vague recollection of a church service that I had attended. The minister must have been particularly eloquent on that Sunday, long ago. Then again, maybe it was just the message that seemed to resonate. What stuck with me was the kindness, gentleness and hopeful message given by Jesus. Blessed are the following; the poor, the meek, the pure in heart, the peacemakers and so forth. What a wonderful message.

As with so many other passages in the Bible, Christians have a way of emphasizing the good and ignoring parts they would rather not speak about. Jesus, on the other hand, spelled it out quite clearly. He was specific in some areas in this sermon. And yet, it appears to me that Christians once again like to cherry pick and veer away from some of the less agreeable teachings of Jesus.

Unlike the church sermons, when the congregation only hears the good, in this section, I analyze the great sermon in its entirety; the good, the bad and the ugly.

Matthew 5: 1-48 King James Version (KJV)

1: *"And seeing the multitudes, he went up into a mountain: and when he was set, his disciples came unto him:"*

2: *"And he opened his mouth, and taught them, saying,"*

I find it strange that upon seeing the multitudes (what is a multitude) let us say 1,000, Jesus decided to go up into a mountain. Why would he go into a mountain, if a thousand people came to hear and see him? I guess we can assume he was in fact on a mountain; as so many seem to represent Jesus on a mountain, rather than in a mountain.

Actually, going up a mountain is not a bad idea as he could stand up and be seen by all. Being the son of God, he would be able to project his voice as if speaking in a microphone, and would be heard by all. Seen by all and heard by all. But this did not happen. Instead Jesus sat down and talked to his disciples. While he was giving this, his longest sermon of record, what were the multitudes doing? They couldn't hear him and they couldn't even see him. The folk, in those days, were not the most educated or disciplined. Can you really see a thousand people just quietly behaving themselves while Jesus decided to have a chat with his disciples? It would be like going to a rock concert today, and the main entertainer decides to play an acoustic guitar to only the front row.

It doesn't seem logical with having a captive audience he would sit down. (ESV: *Seeing the crowds, he went up on the mountain, and when he sat down, his disciples came to him*). The phantom writers of Matthew really blew their opportunity to insert more make-believe stuff into this story.

I would have inserted; *"And when Jesus spoke the multitudes heard every word as if the Lord was speaking to each one."* I guess we will have to wait for the next re-write of the Bible. Has it been ten, or is it twenty re-writes?

3. *"Blessed are the poor in spirit: for theirs is the kingdom of heaven".*

You notice Jesus did not say: *"Blessed are the poor"*; but rather, *"Blessed are the poor in spirit."* This could mean people who are sad, despondent, feeling dejected. Judging from the times of Jesus, many would fit this category. It could also mean those who lack faith. But this would contradict many of his other teachings, for Christians preach only the faithful shall enter the kingdom of heaven. There you have it, even if you have little faith. Yours is the kingdom of heaven. You figure it out.

4. *"Blessed are they that mourn: for they shall be comforted."*

I know many people who have lost their loved ones and experienced painful grief. This is not only a human emotion as we see evidence of mourning in the animal kingdom as well. A touching account of elephants mourning the loss of a young bull is recounted at Elephants without Borders, (registered charity) which shows young elephants 'hugging' the body, and the herd gathering around in silence. I must admit that religion has found a niche in this area of human need. It is not so much a belief in Jesus or God that comforts them, but rather the support of family and friends in a time of personal pain that helps. In times of great personal tragedy or loss; some folks may have nowhere else to turn. They may have no friends or relatives to seek comfort. I must confess that religion can and does serve as a vehicle for grieving.

I submit, in most cases, it is the expression of human compassion and personal empathy, whether that comes from a pastor or friend and family that help those in mourning, rather than any deity.

5. *"Blessed are the meek: for they shall inherit the earth."*

I always thought; boy this is nice; the mild, timid, gentle people are going to inherit the earth. But then I began to think what life on earth would be like after Armageddon.

In Revelation, the Bible gives the most obscene, bizarre and horrible description for the end of times. The way in which it is described, in the Bible, is just too crazy with all kinds of beasts, monsters, angels, and plagues that it requires a separate book. The earth will be a real mess by the time God gets finished with his destructive ways. God will have, in his first go around, killed-off one fourth of the population, and most of the wild animals, by wars, famine and pestilence. There have been at least two gigantic world shaking earthquakes. How many will die isn't recorded.

God just doesn't fire one barrage at the earth, and all its inhabitants, but he keeps firing on all cylinders. This holocaust is nothing like anyone has every seen before. Picture if you will 1,000,000 (1 million) Hiroshima's. Get the picture?

Much of the earth, its life on land and in the sea, will have been wiped out. The oceans and fresh water will be polluted. At a later part it states there will be no need for our sun or moon, and many of the stars, as they can no longer be seen because of the polluted air. And the meek shall inherit the earth. Hey, don't worry, the Lord Jesus will set it all straight for all you meek and mild people. I just love the last two verses of Revelation.

Revelation 22:20-21 New King James Version (NKJV)

20. *"He who testifies to these things says, "Surely I am coming quickly." Amen. Even so, come, Lord Jesus!"*

So, Jesus said; *"I am coming quickly."* You got to be kidding me! 2,000 years and he said he is coming quickly. So he is telling these folks, 2,000 years ago, don't worry I'm coming back quickly. I'll be back to make everything right for you; the good people on earth. Well, we descendants of our descendants are all still waiting. And then, after all this destruction, he says:

21. *"The grace of our Lord Jesus Christ be with you all. Amen."*

The grace of our Lord; what the hell does grace mean? Between Jesus and his father; God, or are they really one and the same; there has been a lot more cruelty, vengeance, torture and destruction than grace. The two of these monsters make a fine pair, throw the Holy Ghost into the mix, and what you have is not the holy trinity but rather the holy terror!

As I lift my face, from the palms of my hands, I shutter. And there are millions of Christian who actually believe, in their lifetime, Jesus is going to return. Every generation of Christians seem to have a special date for the second coming. I got news for them. There is no second coming. In fact there never was a first coming. So get a grip on yourselves and start enjoying this life as there is no afterlife. The only people who are going to inherit the earth will be our children and their children's children and so forth. This has been the case ever since mankind evolved, and will continue to be as long as the human race doesn't destroy itself in the name of religion.

On to the next proclamation in the sermon.

6. "Blessed are they which do hunger and thirst after righteousness: for they shall be filled."

It is to be noted that Jesus is not saying the hungry and thirsty, but rather those who **hunger and thirst after righteousness.** What does Jesus mean by righteousness? I think it is safe to say that acting in accord with divine or moral law, and being free from guilt or sin is how the Bible defines righteousness. Lest there be any confusion, we have many examples of righteous men in the Bible. One example is this fellow Lot, who was willing to turn over his two daughters to be raped by a raging mob. Then later, he got so drunk he supposedly didn't realize he was having sex with his same two daughters. Isn't this a nice example of righteousness?

This is one way you can understand what it means to be righteous. Now you could take Noah as another example of a righteous man; a true family man. Noah also liked to drink to excess. On one of his drunken nights he fell asleep naked. Ham, one of Noah's sons, comes into the tent, sees his father drunk and naked and goes out to tell his two brothers. The two brothers walk in backwards, so as to cover their father without looking at him. Noah wakes up and curses, not only Ham, but Ham's son Canaan. Now that's righteousness.

So all those who hunger and thirst for righteousness, you too could be just like Lot and Noah. You might notice the last five words of this proclamation; *.....*"*for they shall be filled."* Filled with what.....booze? You notice Jesus did not say fulfilled. Now that's just too cute.

7. "Blessed are the merciful: for they shall obtain mercy."

Now we are talking real humanism here. Jesus, my good man, I think you hit the bulls-eye with this one. What does it mean to be merciful? It means to have compassion, to feel and suffer with another person, to be intensely aware of another's pain, and to feel a yearning for their healing. Just like the Good Samaritan; my favourite Bible story.

I'm glad to hear Jesus is going to dispense mercy, because his father doesn't seem to have much. Did you hear what happened to Uzza, some call him Uzzah?

I Chronicles 13: 7 – 11 *"And they carried the ark of God in a new cart out of the house of Abinadab: and Uzza and Ahio drave the cart. And David and all Israel played before God with all their might, and with singing, and with harps, and with psalteries, and with timbrels, and with cymbals, and with trumpets. And when they came unto the threshing floor of Chidon, Uzza put forth his hand to hold the ark; for the oxen stumbled. And the anger of the LORD was kindled against Uzza, and he smote him, because he put his hand to the ark: and there he died before God. And David was displeased, because the LORD had made a breach upon Uzza: wherefore that place is called Perezuzza to this day."*

Ok, so let's recap this story. When David became king, he set out to bring the Ark of the Covenant to Jerusalem. The Ark was placed on a new cart, which was led by Uzza and Ahio, the sons of Abinadab. At the threshing floor of Nacon, something went wrong. The oxen stumbled and almost upset the Ark. Uzza reached out and put his hands on it to steady it. Immediately, God struck Uzza dead for the irreverence of touching the ark.

As you can guess by now this God fellow is quite petulant and reactionary. I'm willing to bet that had Uzza stood by and watched the ark fall and be smashed to pieces, God would have still struck him dead. Uzza's death is one of the most discussed executions of the Bible. It seems rather unfair to kill someone who's had taken care of the Ark for twenty years and who probably grew up with it. But on the other hand, when it comes to God, you don't fool about. God just loves to find any opportunity to do some killing.

David's gets upset with God for killing Uzza. After all, David and his friends were singing and dancing, and God's vengeance spoiled the happy homecoming of the Ark. It's a wonder David wasn't struck down for displaying his anger with God. The place where this happened was dubbed, by David, as Perez-uzza. Uzza means strong and perez means to break. One can interpret this to mean: *'break the strong'*. David is pushing his luck here by trying God's patience. Ah, yes; God the merciful.

8. *"Blessed are the pure in heart: for they shall see God."*

The first part of this proclamation is good stuff. I believe *'pure in heart'* simply means being a good person or someone without malice, treachery, or evil intent; honest; sincere; guileless. The second part is curious. I'm not sure who, if anyone can see God. As usual we discover mixed messages in the Bible.

Genesis 17:1 *"Now when Abram was ninety-nine years old, the LORD appeared to Abram and said to him, "I am God Almighty; Walk before Me, and be blameless;"*

Gen. 18:1 *"Now the LORD appeared to him by the oaks of Mamre, while he was sitting at the tent door in the heat of the day."*

Exodus 6:2-3 *"God spoke further to Moses and said to him, "I am the LORD; *and I appeared to Abraham, Isaac, and Jacob, as God Almighty, but by My name, LORD, I did not make Myself known to them."*

*This is strange syntax. In most Bible passages whoever is the writer refers to God in the third person. In this passage it is as though God himself wrote it?

Exodus 24:9-11 *"Then Moses went up with Aaron, Nadab and Abihu, and seventy of the elders of Israel, and they saw the God of Israel; and under His feet there appeared to be a pavement of sapphire, as clear as the sky itself. Yet He did not stretch out His hand against the nobles of the sons of Israel; and they saw God, and they ate and drank."*

Num. 12:6-8 *"He said, "Hear now My words: If there is a prophet among you, I, the LORD, shall make Myself known to him in a vision. I shall speak with him in a dream. "Not so, with My servant Moses, He is faithful in all My household; With him I speak mouth to mouth, Even openly, and not in dark sayings, And he beholds the form of the LORD. Why then were you not afraid to speak against My servant, against Moses?"*

So there you have it, God appeared before these folks; they must have been pure in heart. How then are we to understand the following passages in the Bible?

Exodus 33:20 *"But He [God] said, "You cannot see My face, for no man can see Me and live!"*

John 1:18 *"No one has seen God at any time; the only begotten God who is in the bosom of the Father, He has explained Him."*

John 5:37 *"And the Father who sent Me, He has testified of Me. You have neither heard His voice at any time nor seen His form."*

John 6:46 *"Not that anyone has seen the Father, except the One who is from God; He has seen the Father."*

1 Tim. 6:15-16 *"He who is the blessed and only Sovereign, the King of kings and Lord of lords, who alone possesses immortality and dwells in unapproachable light, whom no man has seen or can see. To Him be honour and eternal dominion! Amen."*

Far be it from me to say, (with my tongue firmly in my cheek) this is a contradiction as we have already learned the Bible is a model of consistency. Go figure?

9. *"Blessed are the peacemakers: for they shall be called the children of God."*

It is nice that the peacemakers are being blessed. By the way 'blessed' to religious folks seem to mean some kind of divine comfort; when really it means a wish of happiness, contentment or joy.

As far as being called the children of God, considering the way God has treated children in the Bible, I'm not sure I want to be around this monster. We have already read earlier in this book how God treats children in general and in particular how he arranged the beating and crucifixion of his own son.

In the book, **'The Born Again Skeptic's Guide to the Bible'** Ruth Hurmence Green states the following on page 307.

"The Bible is fertile ground for all who might wish, for any reason, to employ extreme severity, if not actual abuse, in the treatment of children.

Adults who want to beat their children find no reason to refrain from corporal punishment when they go to the scriptures, and they are even instructed to whip them mercilessly. One irate parent or guardian with a Bible is all it takes to inflict pain to the point of death upon an unruly or "stubborn" child:

Proverbs 23: 13-14 *"Withhold not correction from the child: for if thou beatest him with the rod, he shall not die. Thou shalt beat him with the rod, and shalt deliver his soul from hell."*

But as history books and modern newspapers attest, many children have died, especially when the Bible-inspired beating was performed by the reader who turned to **Proverbs 20.30:** *"The blueness of the wound cleanesth away evil: so do stripes the inward parts of the belly." An ungentle Dr. Spock of Proverbs is responsible for "Spare the rod and spoil the child."*

"Honour thy father and thy mother; that thy days may be long upon land," etc.: **Exodus 20:12,** *was to be taken literally. Honour was to be bestowed, not because it had been earned, but to save the child's very life. Not only were smiting and cursing capital offences when perpetrated against a parent, but should children be stubborn or espouse a "false doctrine," fathers and mothers were to stone them to death or run them through with a sword. At one time a "stubborn child" statute in Massachusetts evolved from this Mosaic Law."*

If you want to be one of the Children of God, I'm tempted to say; *"God help you."* But I think that is the last place I would look for help.

10-12 *"Blessed are they which are persecuted for righteousness' sake: for theirs is the kingdom of heaven. Blessed are ye, when men shall revile you, and persecute you, and shall say all manner of evil against you falsely, for my sake. Rejoice, and be exceeding glad: for great is your reward in heaven: for so persecuted they the prophets which were before you."*

This is an interesting proclamation. Here we have a demonstration of the arrogance of God, Jesus and subsequently the Christian religion. I remember so well timid people challenging the Catholic Church as their priests molest innocent children. Some were viciously counter-attacked by the church.

Many religious parents whose children told the truth to their mothers and fathers, of what the priests did to them, were physically punished and sent to their room. They were told to pray for forgiveness for the outrages things they said. In other words, never challenge the church, the Bible, God or Jesus. Anything that is said, written or done, from these sources is to go unchallenged.

Any kind of challenge, questioning or expression of doubt is viewed as persecution. Remember the Inquisition? In some religions you are still subject to torture and death should you have the audacity to challenge them? Christianity has mellowed somewhat from the days of the Inquisition. Physical torture and death has been replaced with psychological and emotional torture. Some so-called Christian sects will shun and disown anyone who thinks for themselves.

This proclamation by Jesus is one that religious fanatics cling to. It helps to nurture their faith beyond all reason. This is where believers get the idea that atheists, humanists and other non-believers are evil people. Why are we evil? We have the nerve to challenge, question and confront their superstitious beliefs. Once fanatics believe, with such religious fervour, it is impossible to have any kind of reasonable or sane dialogue.

13-16 *"Ye are the salt of the earth: but if the salt have lost his savour, wherewith shall it be salted? It is thenceforth good for nothing, but to be cast out, and to be trodden under foot of men. Ye are the light of the world. A city that is set on a hill cannot be hid. Neither do men light a candle, and put it under a bushel, but on a candlestick; and it giveth light unto all that are in the house. Let your light so shine before men, that they may see your good works, and glorify your Father which is in heaven."*

Salt is a preservative, so in other words you must preserve the message. Light is to spread the word. Here is where Christians get the idea that the word of God is good and that it must be preserved and spread all over the world...just like a virus. Once this virus infects the people, the antidote, for some, is never found. I hope this book provides the antidote for some that have been infected, but have not yet become fatal.

17-20 *"Think not that I am come to destroy the law, or the prophets: I am not come to destroy, but to fulfil. For verily I say unto you, Till heaven and earth pass, one jot or one title shall in no wise pass from the law, till all be fulfilled. Whosoever therefore shall break one of these least commandments, and shall teach men so, he shall be called the least in the kingdom of heaven:*

but whosoever shall do and teach them, the same shall be called great in the kingdom of heaven. For I say unto you, that except your righteousness shall exceed the righteousness of the scribes and Pharisees, ye shall in no case enter into the kingdom of heaven."

Most Christians are hypocrites. These four verses are among the most powerful of the proclamations Jesus made during the famous Sermon. Yet, most Christian preachers spend little time explaining them to the congregation. They prefer to ignore much of the Old Testament and then cherry-pick from the New Testament. Here is one cherry that should be picked....and fully explained. Christian followers will not get a full explanation in any church service of these, supposedly, Christ's words. Let me try.

The first line is powerful. What Jesus said is that everything in the Old Testament, which is set down by God or his prophets is the Law! And let there be no misunderstanding, he told everyone that he came to fulfill the laws of the Old Testament.

To emphasize this point he said not one jot shall be deviated until every law has been followed. And if anyone needed further clarification as just what he meant, he went on to say that anyone who shall break even the **least** of these laws or commandments they will be called the least in the kingdom of heaven. Additionally, if you don't meet his criteria of righteousness; you are not getting into heaven.

Every good Christian knows the laws, so you had better follow them. I am told that Moses alone gave some six hundred laws for the Israelites to follow. I really don't know how many laws Christians are supposed to follow; but in case you forgot, here is a little refresher course on just a few of them.

- Don't work on the Sabbath.
- No sex outside of marriage (adultery).
- Even if you think (lust) about having sex with someone, you have committed adultery. (Oops, I'm getting ahead of myself verses 27-28)
- If your mouthy teenager talks back to you; you are to stone him/her to death.
- Never lie (God and Jesus never made any exceptions for the little white lies).
- Don't steal (Not even a pencil from work).
- Don't swear (God Damn it!).
- Oh! I forgot the 2nd. Commandment. Let me revise my earlier statement that most Christians are hypocrites; nay, all Christians are hypocrites.

I am beginning to think that this so-called place, known as heaven, is going to be rather desolate and lonely.

21-24 *"Ye have heard that it was said of them of old time, Thou shalt not kill; and whosoever shall kill shall be in danger of the judgment: But I say unto you, That whosoever is angry with his brother without a cause shall be in danger of the judgment: and whosoever shall say to his brother, Raca, shall be in danger of the council: but whosoever shall say, Thou fool, shall be in danger of hell fire. Therefore if thou bring thy gift to the altar, and there rememberest that thy brother hath ought against thee; Leave there thy gift before the altar, and go thy way; first be reconciled to thy brother, and then come and offer thy gift."*

Let us use plain English and try to simplify this one.

Basically, Jesus is saying killing is still wrong, but even if you get angry or threaten someone without cause, you are in danger of being judged as being the same as a killer. However, if you make amends with your brother (friend, neighbour, whatever) and leave a little something for the church, all will be forgiven. Nice eh!

25-26 *"Agree with thine adversary quickly, whiles thou art in the way with him; lest at any time the adversary deliver thee to the judge, and the judge deliver thee to the officer, and thou be cast into prison. Verily I say unto thee, Thou shalt by no means come out thence, till thou hast paid the uttermost farthing."*

Now here is a good piece of advice. More people should follow this and we would all be the better for it. Being an arbitrator and mediator, there is good reason to stay out of court. First of all court is financially costly. Second, it often takes a long time to get your matter resolved. Thirdly, it is very stressful. And finally, when it is all over there is usually one so-called winner and one loser. The end result may leave hard feelings that can often result in the loser seeking some kind of retribution, and further problems can surface which may result in more litigation.

On the second part; if you are judged and thrown into jail, accept it, serve your time or pay your fine. I would have added however, that you should say no more of your disagreement and leave it alone and get on with your life.

I don't know what this has to do with God or religion, but this is at least one area where atheists, aka humanists and religion can agree. Our human activities into matters of everyday life call upon all of us to reconcile matters with those we have disagreements. It makes sense to reconcile quickly before folks get into any legal proceedings.

27-28 *"Ye have heard that it was said by them of old time, Thou shalt not commit adultery: But I say unto you, That whosoever looketh on a woman to lust after her hath committed adultery with her already in his heart."*

Remember this one? I find it curious. It appears to be only intended for males. I guess females that lust after men are exempt from this order. At any rate, any of you lusting males, I guess you qualify as an adulterer. This should include quite a few Christians.

29-30 *"And if thy right eye offend thee, pluck it out, and cast it from thee: for it is profitable for thee that one of thy members should perish, and not that thy whole body should be cast into hell. And if thy right hand offend thee, cut it off, and cast it from thee: for it is profitable for thee that one of thy members should perish, and not that thy whole body should be cast into hell."*

This can be a scary passage, even for adults. It is no doubt confusing. If you look for a religious interpretation you may read this to mean if parts of you are sinning, stop it.

Closer to reality, it could mean if you have an illness or disease with a body part, cut it out or cut it off, so that the rest of your body is not infected. At any rate, Jesus Christ likes to talk in riddles. It is a curious way to deliver messages.

The problem with this passage; the person with one arm is deformed or defective. If this is so, then God apparently doesn't want these people to come anywhere near God's sanctuary. I don't know how Christians square this passage with the following passage?

Lev.21:17-23 *"Speak unto Aaron, saying , Whosoever he be of thy seed in their generations that hath any blemish, let him not approach to offer the bread of his God. For whatsoever man he be that hath a blemish, he shall not approach : a blind man, or a lame, or he that hath a flat nose , or any thing superfluous , Or a man that is brokenfooted , or brokenhanded , Or crookbackt, or a dwarf, or that hath a blemish in his eye, or be scurvy, or scabbed, or hath his stones broken; No man that hath a blemish of the seed of Aaron the priest shall come nigh to offer the offerings of the LORD made by fire: he hath a blemish; he shall not come nigh to offer the bread of his God. He shall eat the bread of his God, both of the most holy, and of the holy. Only he shall not go in unto the vail, nor come nigh unto the altar, because he hath a blemish; that he profane not my sanctuaries: for I the LORD do sanctify them. And Moses told it unto Aaron, and to his sons, and unto all the children of Israel."*

This is indeed a strange passage. I suppose one could read this as being applicable only to priests, and further, only those who are descendants of Aaron. OK, all you disfigured priests, get busy and start checking your ancestry.

31-32 *"It hath been said, Whosoever shall put away his wife, let him give her a writing of divorcement: But I say unto you, That whosoever shall put away his wife, saving for the cause of fornication, causeth her to commit adultery: and whosoever shall marry her that is divorced committeth adultery."*

"Adultery" meant unfaithfulness to one's spouse, and any remarriage is adulterous; because in God's sight the original couple remains married. It can't be any clearer.

If you are divorced you can't get remarried, otherwise you are breaking God's commandment. Now we have a few more million Christians that will have to answer to God.

33-37 *"Again, ye have heard that it hath been said by them of old time, Thou shalt not forswear thyself, but shalt perform unto the Lord thine oaths: But I say unto you, Swear not at all; neither by heaven; for it is God's throne: Nor by the earth; for it is his footstool: neither by Jerusalem; for it is the city of the great King. Neither shalt thou swear by thy head, because thou canst not make one hair white or black. But let your communication be, Yea, yea; Nay, nay: for whatsoever is more than these cometh of evil."*

Now this one has really got to grab you by the genitals. How many people swear on the holy Bible in court? How many presidents swear on the Bible when taking office? How many Christians insist on swearing on the Bible as an indication of their truthfulness? Some even kiss the Bible!

Jesus said; stop taking oaths in the name of God as your witness. The point of this passage is integrity. Jesus observes that since God witnesses every word you say anyway, you should be able to tell the truth without having to call God to witness your testimony. Jesus is addressing the abuse of oaths by protecting the sanctity of God's name. Jesus says, just tell the truth; a simple yes or no will do, otherwise you are inviting evil.

There are times when I like this Jesus fellow!

I want all you Christians to consider the words of Jesus when you swear on the Bible.

38-42 *"Ye have heard that it hath been said, An eye for an eye, and a tooth for a tooth: But I say unto you, That ye resist not evil: but whosoever shall smite thee on thy right cheek, turn to him the other also. And if any man will sue thee at the law, and take away thy coat, let him have thy cloak also. And whosoever shall compel thee to go a mile, go with him twain. Give to him that asketh thee, and from him that would borrow of thee turn not thou away."*

Oh boy! I'm not sure the father and son are speaking the same language here? God just loves to kill people, but here Jesus is saying turn the other cheek. God said thou shall not steal. However if one can steal your coat by going to court, you are supposed to not only give up your coat, but give him your cloak as well. And don't forget to go that extra mile. Finally, anyone who wants to borrow from you; you must give it to them.

I really must ask how many Christians actually follow these rules? Just asking? I guess old Shakespeare was at odds with Jesus when he wrote Hamlet. One of the characters in this play, Polonius, advised his immature son the following:

Polonius: *"Neither a borrower nor a lender be: for loan oft loses both itself and friend, and borrowing dulls the edge of husbandry."*

So here we have the logical father advising his son. Listen son, lending money to friends is risky, because hitching debt onto personal relationships can cause resentment and, in the case of default, you can lose both your money and your friend. Borrowing invites more private dangers: it replaces domestic thrift and personal responsibility, with reckless indulgences.

Who to believe: the son of God or some English playwright?

43-48 *"Ye have heard that it hath been said, Thou shalt love thy neighbour, and hate thine enemy. But I say unto you, Love your enemies, bless them that curse you, do good to them that hate you, and pray for them which despitefully use you, and persecute you; That ye may be the children of your Father which is in heaven: for he maketh his sun to rise on the evil and on the good, and sendeth rain on the just and on the unjust. For if ye love them which love you, what reward have ye? Do not even the publicans the same? And if ye salute your brethren only, what do ye more than others? Do not even the publicans so? Be ye therefore perfect, even as your Father which is in heaven is perfect."*

OK, you Christians, if you think you have already been challenged so far; try living up to these commands of Jesus. How many of you love your enemy and pray for those that hate you? I know some Christians who spread love to their enemies. These extreme Islamists ended up kidnapping your fellow Christians and cut their heads off.

I'm the first to admit that I'm not perfect and I don't expect I will ever be perfect. However Jesus is telling all you Christians to be perfect. Good luck!

This concludes Matthew 5. If you have followed all of what Jesus has prescribed so far you may look something like this; if you are meek, you will inherit a world that has been desecrated, polluted and destroyed of most life; but don't worry Jesus is coming quickly. If you are righteous you will be filled. We know what it means to be righteous, but being filled, that's another question. If you are pure in heart, you might see God, then again you might not. If you are a peacemaker, you will be treated like a child. As long as you spread the word, you will be blessed. You will not be divorced, you won't work on Sunday.

By now you should have stoned all your children to death, and you will not go to church as you can't pray to or make any graven image of anything in heaven. You will never be angry with anyone. Sorry, no nooky on the side and don't even think about it. And you should be broke, without clothes, love everyone and be perfect. Nice eh?

Matthew 6: 1-34 (KJV)

1-4 *"Beware of practicing your piety before men in order to be seen by them; for then you will have no reward from your Father who is in heaven. Thus, when you give alms, sound no trumpet before you, as the hypocrites do in the synagogues and in the streets, that they may be praised by men. Truly, I say to you, they have received their reward. But when you give alms, do not let your left hand know what your right hand is doing. So that your alms may be in secret; and your Father who sees in secret will reward you."*

Jesus surely could not be misunderstood. Any good person, who is humble, kind and not wrapped in his own ego, knows what is meant here. In other words, when you give to charity, or the church, you give quietly, in secret and don't go around bragging about it. You don't make a public display of your charity. Yet most religions, including the Christians, violate this command by Jesus. The most flagrant violators, may I suggest, are the evangelists with the television-evangelists having perfected the art of fleecing their flock.

Once again, the hypocrites both give and take in public, brag in public and trumpet their generosity. The so-called messengers of Christ eagerly take this money and bathe in the lap of luxury; and it is all legal.

Furthermore, much of this pilfering of the delusional is further subsidized by all the taxpayers. This rip-off, from the public purse and members of their own congregations, in Christ's name is appalling. Oh! Jesus, will you forgive them....for they know exactly what they do?

5-8 *"And when you pray, you must not be like the hypocrites; for they love to stand and pray in the synagogues and at the street corners, that they may be seen by men. Truly, I say to you, they have received their reward." But when you pray, go into your room and shut the door and pray to your Father who is in secret; and your Father who sees in secret will reward you. And in praying do not heap up empty phrases as the Gentiles do; for they think that they will be heard for their many words. Do not be like them, for your Father knows what you need before you ask him."*

How many Christian religions totally ignore this direction by Jesus in every church, chapel and cathedral each Sunday? Dare I say virtually all? Could Jesus not have been any more clear and concise in his order? His declaration that prayer is a private matter is violated by every Christian around the globe. Who, therefore, are the hypocrites?

Christian apologists can contort, revise and do linguistic somersaults regarding this passage, but there is no escaping the meaning, intent or context in which Jesus describes how people should pray. Yet Christians ignore this directive. Their actions are a blatant violation of how this passage would be understood by any half-wit. Without relying on any other possible intent or assumptions about this passage; Christians are indeed hypocrites. The Pope, with his massive audiences, is the biggest hypocrite of all.

9-13 *"After this manner therefore pray ye: Our Father which art in heaven, Hallowed be thy name. Thy kingdom come, Thy will be done in earth, as it is in heaven. Give us this day our daily bread. And forgive us our debts, as we forgive our debtors. And lead us not into temptation, but deliver us from evil: For thine is the kingdom, and the power, and the glory, for ever. Amen."*

14-15 *"For if ye forgive men their trespasses, your heavenly Father will also forgive you: But if ye forgive not men their trespasses, neither will your Father forgive your trespasses."*

Here we go again, Jesus expressing a very nice way of praying, if one believes in prayer. I can't find too much to criticize here. Pardon my suspicions; but I can't help but wonder how many Christians go through a ritual of saying these words every Sunday in church, and then immediately forgetting their meaning? There are probably some good Christians who do in fact forgive those who trespass upon them. I don't know that you need to be Christian or even religious to understand the benefits of forgiveness. So this is a good thing. As far as this daily bread thing goes; I rather think you should thank the farmer, the baker, and the grocer for giving us our daily bread.

16-18 *"Moreover when ye fast, be not, as the hypocrites, of a sad countenance: for they disfigure their faces, that they may appear unto men to fast. Verily I say unto you, They have their reward. But thou, when thou fastest, anoint thine head, and wash thy face; That thou appear not unto men to fast, but unto thy Father which is in secret: and thy Father, which seeth in secret, shall reward thee openly."*

Once again, Jesus is basically saying don't be a show-off when you fast. This is good advice, so keep yourself cleaned-up and don't go around dishevelled. Judging from the waist and butt size of many folks, a little fasting might help them shed a few unwanted pounds.

19-21 *"Lay not up for yourselves treasures upon earth, where moth and rust doth corrupt, and where thieves break through and steal: But lay up for yourselves treasures in heaven, where neither moth nor rust doth corrupt, and where thieves do not break through nor steal: For where your treasure is, there will your heart be also."*

Could it be any clearer? All you rich Christians have been told; (actually I think your friend Jesus had said this kind of thing a few times) get rid of all your money and belongings. This means your cottage, vacation home in Florida, your second or third car…well you get the idea. Here is a suggestion; give it all to the church, for as Jesus says, your treasure is in heaven. So stop collecting earthly possessions, be like Jesus, and go around in sack-cloth and sandals.

22-23 *"The light of the body is the eye: if therefore thine eye be single, thy whole body shall be full of light. But if thine eye be evil, thy whole body shall be full of darkness. If therefore the light that is in thee be darkness, how great is that darkness!"*

There he goes again, talking in riddles. Why can't this Jesus fellow just spell it out for us simpletons? After all, wasn't he speaking to illiterate folks who for the most part could not read, write, understand philosophy, mathematics and had no concept of physics?

People can have a whole lot of fun trying to interpret this one. I tend to think it has little to do with our eyes.

Rather, it is how we see life. We can either see life through a prism of good or a prism of evil. You can choose to follow good (light) or choose to follow evil (darkness). No doubt here, we would all be better off being good. Sorry to make this sound too simple.

24 *"No man can serve two masters: for either he will hate the one, and love the other; or else he will hold to the one, and despise the other. Ye cannot serve God and mammon."*

I wonder how many people know what the word **"mammon"** means. Throughout this book I admitted my ignorance. I have, or should I say had, no idea what this word meant. This is the kind of Bible passage one would read and just move on, without thinking any further about the word mammon. Initially, I thought this meant "man". Thus the passage meant you cannot serve two masters; meaning God and man. You must choose one or the other. However, I was wrong.

Apparently the word mammon means wealth or riches; for sake of argument, let us call it money. Now here again, the Lord Jesus Christ is telling all good Christians about the evils of money. You cannot serve God and money. I would venture to guess that most, not all, but most Christians spend a lot more time thinking about money than they do thinking about God. Do I have any data or evidence to back-up this statement? None at all. As I've said many times before, this book is about my opinions which often lack intensive research.

Speaking about research. Apparently; scholars are at odds about the source of the word mammon. While it appears here in Matthew 6:24 of the Bible, and also in some verses of Luke, it is a word hard to find elsewhere.

In the 4th century writings the word "mammon" shows up. Does it mean this passage in Matthew wasn't written until the 4th century? Perhaps it was edited in the 4th century by some priest? Who knows? We do know that new words are brought into languages all the time. It is, however, curious to note. Is it possible that Jesus never used the word mammon at all? Just asking?

Alright folks, let us pause for a moment and just think about all what Jesus has said up to this point. I want all you good Christians to ask yourself this question. Are you honestly and truly following his teachings? Can you answer this question truthfully?

I now want you to buckle up your seat belts. You may just fall off your chair after reading the last few verses of Matthew 6. If you happen to have a devout Christian financial advisor, perhaps you should seek his advice.

25 *"Therefore I say unto you, Take no thought for your life, what ye shall eat, or what ye shall drink; nor yet for your body, what ye shall put on. Is not the life more than meat, and the body than raiment?"*

26-29 *"Behold the fowls of the air: for they sow not, neither do they reap, nor gather into barns; yet your heavenly Father feedeth them. Are ye not much better than they? Which of you by taking thought can add one cubit unto his stature? And why take ye thought for raiment? Consider the lilies of the field, how they grow; they toil not, neither do they spin:* <u>*And yet I say unto you, That even Solomon in all his glory was not arrayed like one of these.*</u>*"*

30-31 *"Wherefore, if God so clothe the grass of the field,*
which to day is, and to morrow is cast into the oven, **shall**
he *not much more* **clothe** *you, O ye of little faith?*
Therefore take no thought, saying, What shall we eat? or,
What shall we drink? or, Wherewithal shall we be
clothed?"

32-34 *"(For after all these things do the Gentiles seek:)*
for your heavenly Father knoweth that ye have need of all
these things. But seek ye first the kingdom of God, and
his righteousness; and all these things shall be added
unto you. Take therefore no thought for the morrow: for
the morrow shall take thought for the things of itself.
Sufficient unto the day **is** *the evil thereof."*

Jesus gets a bit repetitious in these verses. In this section of
Matthew; Christians, trying to interpret these verses, are
like the performers in a circus. They jump through hoops,
make elephants disappear, and play word games to
reconcile their lifestyle with the teachings of Jesus. Let us
try to figure out exactly what Jesus is saying here. I don't
think he is saying to go around totally naked. I'll give
Christians a little slack here. However, we do have some
contradictions. Jesus is saying don't be like the Gentiles.
Well, who are the Gentiles? Basically, it is anyone who is
not Jewish. So Christians are Gentiles. But Christ was a
Jew. Rather confusing isn't it?

Let me try to understand this. Gentiles think about
tomorrow and whether they will have food, drink and
clothes. But if you follow Christ, all these things will be
provided.....somehow. He talks about the lilies of the field
who toil not and God takes care of them. OK, so all you
Christian lilies don't think too much about tomorrow as
God will take care of you.

And what the heck is this statement about Solomon: "***And yet I say unto you, That even Solomon in all his glory was not arrayed like one of these.***" Huh? King Solomon, with his 1,000 wives, living in the lap of luxury and toying with other gods? I don't get it? Maybe Jesus was talking about a different Solomon.

Quite frankly, I think Jesus is giving out some bad advice here. Don't give any thought about tomorrow is not a good idea. Don't think about what to eat, drink, or if you have clothes, is not too wise. While preachers and priests may wax eloquently about the Beatitudes, not many preach to their flock to "take no thought of tomorrow."

Matthew 7: 1-29 (KJV)

1-2 *"Judge not, that ye be not judged. For with what judgment ye judge, ye shall be judged: and with what measure ye mete, it shall be measured to you again."*

I would think this is fairly clear and understandable. I wonder how many Christians actually follow this edict. There are times I feel as though religious folks are constantly judging others. This is one of the problems of religion. I find they are indeed judgemental.

It is toxic to evaluate the behaviour and problems of others in the context of religious beliefs. Religious dogma almost requires one to judge others in every aspect of life, as defined by the scriptures. However, Jesus seems to be saying be very careful with your judgments. People should consider their own weaknesses and action very carefully before making judgments on others. Condemning someone else, when you may have even bigger problems or behaviour in your life, is hypocrisy.

3-5 *"And why beholdest thou the mote that is in thy brother's eye, but considerest not the beam that is in thine own eye? Or how wilt thou say to thy brother, Let me pull out the mote out of thine eye; and, behold, a beam is in thine own eye? Thou hypocrite, first cast out the beam out of thine own eye; and then shalt thou see clearly to cast out the mote out of thy brother's eye."*

Many Christians seem to interpret the above verses literally. I believe it has nothing to do with a speck in anyone's eyes. Rather Jesus is saying correct your own flaws first before going about correcting others. Otherwise, you are a hypocrite. I would suggest we have plenty of religious hypocrites who do not see their own flaws.

6 *"Give not that which is holy unto the dogs, neither cast ye your pearls before swine, lest they trample them under their feet, and turn again and rend you."*

I believe Jesus is talking about me, and those like me. He calls me a dog and a swine. I rather like dogs, and swine is quite tasty if cooked properly. To all you Christians; don't waste your pearls of wisdom on me as I will rend or slash them. Yes indeed. That is exactly the purpose of this book. I hope to demonstrate just how you have been fooled into believing this fairy tale of God, Jesus and the Holy Bible.

7-8 *"Ask, and it shall be given you; seek, and ye shall find; knock, and it shall be opened unto you: For every one that asketh receiveth; and he that seeketh findeth; and to him that knocketh it shall be opened."*

I have a news flash for all the millions of starving, dying, suffering people who have been asking Jesus, and his Dad, for help, but are never heard. This is the most horrible joke to play on the millions of people who ask, but never receive.

9-14 *"Or what man is there of you, whom if his son ask bread, will he give him a stone? Or if he ask a fish, will he give him a serpent? If ye then, being evil, know how to give good gifts unto your children, how much more shall your Father which is in heaven give good things to them that ask him? Therefore all things whatsoever ye would that men should do to you, do ye even so to them: for this is the law and the prophets. Enter ye in at the strait gate: for wide* is *the gate, and broad* is *the way, that leadeth to destruction, and many there be which go in thereat: Because strait* is *the gate, and narrow* is *the way, which leadeth unto life, and few there be that find it."*

How could anyone disagree with this? Certainly, if someone asks for bread, you are not going to give him a stone, etc. However, I know of many people who asked for help from the so-called Father in heaven and received only bad things in their life. So Jesus is basically saying the route to heaven is not easy, you need to follow the straight and narrow. Interesting how the verse ends *"and few there be that find it."*

I am sure there are a lot more Christians, than there is room in heaven, who think they are among the lucky few.

15 *"Beware of false prophets, which come to you in sheep's clothing, but inwardly they are ravening wolves."*

Just who are the false prophets? First of all we must begin by understanding what is a prophet? In religion, a *prophet* is an individual who claims, if not contacted by the supernatural or the divine; at least he speaks for God. He serves as an intermediary with humanity, delivering this newfound knowledge from the supernatural entity to other people. OK, now what is a false prophet?

A **false prophet** is simply someone who speaks for another but **falsely**. **False prophets** either speak for the wrong god, or they claim to have heard from the true God but do not accurately represent Him or His words. Got it?

Let me explain. If you are Christian; then a Muslim, or a Jew or a Hindu all are false prophets. But it gets a bit more complicated. If you are a Catholic Christian then a Presbyterian or Baptist Christian, is a false prophet. Now since there are some 30,000+ Christian denominations we have at least that many false prophets plus all the other religious denominations.

In other words whatever religion you belong to must be the right one, and all the others are led by false prophets. So watch out for those ravening wolves. Isn't that nice?

16-20 *"Ye shall know them by their fruits. Do men gather grapes of thorns, or figs of thistles? Even so every good tree bringeth forth good fruit; but a corrupt tree bringeth forth evil fruit. A good tree cannot bring forth evil fruit, neither* **can** *a corrupt tree bring forth good fruit. Every tree that bringeth not forth good fruit is hewn down, and cast into the fire. Wherefore by their fruits ye shall know them."*

I think this riddle is easy to decipher. Jesus is saying be good and you can tell the good folk from the bad folk by their deeds. Not too profound.

Now what happens to the bad ones? They are cut down and cast into the fire. Jesus said he was coming back quickly. It has only been 2,000 years and he hasn't returned yet....but you better watch out! It's a simple message: just like Santa Claus, so remember this:

You better watch out, you better not cry
Better not pout, I'm telling you why
Jesus Christ is comin' to town
He's making a list and checking it twice
Gonna find out who's naughty and nice
Jesus Christ is comin' to town
He sees you when you're a sleepin'
He knows when you're awake
He knows if you've been bad or good
So be good for goodness sake
Oh! You better watch out, you better not cry
Better not pout, I'm telling you why
Jesus Christ is comin' to town.

21-23 *"Not every one that saith unto me, Lord, Lord, shall enter into the kingdom of heaven; but he that doeth the will of my Father which is in heaven. Many will say to me in that day, Lord, Lord, have we not prophesied in thy name? and in thy name have cast out devils? and in thy name done many wonderful works? And then will I profess unto them, I never knew you: depart from me, ye that work iniquity."*

Jesus gets a bit repetitious. He reminds us that not every one gets into heaven, but only those who do his bidding. The rest of you heathens: *"get away from me."* To emphasize his point he uses the following nice little parable; either you build your house strong or you get blown away.

24-27 *"Therefore whosoever heareth these sayings of mine, and doeth them, I will liken him unto a wise man, which built his house upon a rock: And the rain descended, and the floods came, and the winds blew, and beat upon that house; and it fell not: for it was founded upon a rock.*

And every one that heareth these sayings of mine, and doeth them not, shall be likened unto a foolish man, which built his house upon the sand: And the rain descended, and the floods came, and the winds blew, and beat upon that house; and it fell: and great was the fall of it."

28-29 *"And it came to pass, when Jesus had ended these sayings, <u>the people were astonished</u> at his doctrine: For he taught them as* **one** *having authority, and not as the scribes."*

I'm astonished too. I'm more astonished that the people were astonished as only a handful sitting in front of him would have heard anything he said.

Of all that is written in the Bible; Christians simply gush over the Sermon on the Mount. Grant it, there are some very good messages. It is interesting how they cherry pick the good words and ignore the bad and ugly words of Christ; words that would make most Christians red-faced. I have yet to read a book, website or listen to a podcast that challenged the **entire** Sermon on the Mount.

I know most Christians, and other religions, have no sense of humour when their religion is criticized or ridiculed. The time has come when all religions deserve to be ridiculed, when appropriate. I also have no problem in praising religion when credit is their due. The Sermon on the Mount, as I said in the beginning of this critique; has its good, bad and ugly.

I don't want to be accused of plagiarism, but apparently there is someone out there that has accused Jesus of plagiarism.

You may read it in its entirety by going to the website Christianity Revealed at: http://jdstone.org/cr/index.html I have reprinted a portion of this information as found and without any comments from me. You can decide for yourself on its veracity.

THE SERMON ON THE MOUNT

Edited by John Stone

In the New Testament, the unknown author of Matthew, in chapters 5-7, has Jesus — invisible man in the sky/god incarnate — showcasing his "wisdom" in the famous *"Sermon on the Mount."* How original was Jesus' so-called wisdom? Was this something "new" that Jesus was bringing to the people? Or was Jesus just reciting long established Jewish teachings?

Here are some examples that pre-date Jesus.

Proverbs 29:23 ‖ ...he who is lowly in spirit shall obtain honor.

Psalms 147:3 ‖ He heals the brokenhearted, and binds up their wounds.

Psalms 37:11 ‖ The meek shall inherit the earth, and delight themselves in the abundance of peace.

Psalms 24:3--4 || Who shall ascend the mount of the Lord, and who shall stand in His holy place? He who has clean hands and a pure heart...

Lamentations 3:30 || Let him offer his cheek to him who smites him....

Proverbs 25:21 || If your enemy is hungry, give him bread to eat, and if he is thirsty, give him water to drink....

Psalms 37:4 || Delight yourself in the Lord, and He shall give you the desires of your heart.

Jeremiah 29:13 || You shall seek Me and find Me when you search for Me with all your heart.

Psalms 6:9 || Depart from me, all you workers of evil...

"As you can clearly see, the "pious fraud" and "plagiarism" of Matthew — the unknown New Testament author of the first book of the Christian bible — is clearly evident! Even as the Christian writers, editors and copyists were depicting Jews as lowly degenerates, the pearls of Jewish wisdom were being stolen and attributed to the imaginary man-god Jesus aka Invisible Man in the Sky!" **-John Stone**

As George Constanza, that great American sage, once said:

"Remember Jerry, it's not a lie if you really believe it's true."

Final Award

"The Bible is one of the greatest blessings bestowed by God on the children of men. It has God for its author; salvation for its end, and truth without any mixture for its matter. It is all pure." **-John Locke**

"The Bible has noble poetry in it... and some good morals and a wealth of obscenity, and upwards of a thousand lies."   **-Mark Twain**

Note to the Reader: What follows is a mock arbitration. The names of the parties are fictitious. The location of the arbitration is a fabrication. It is written for the lay person, and does not entirely follow the normal protocols fitting of a properly written decision. I have taken some liberty in an effort to make this final award more readable for the ordinary person. A properly worded arbitration decision, like a court decision, would be too dry and technical for the purposes of this book.

I have however attempted to give it some of the look and feel of an actual arbitration decision. An actual decision covering such a big question would be several hundreds of pages in length. This decision has been severely truncated.

In the matter of an Arbitration, pursuant to the Arbitration Act, 1991, SO 1991, c 17

(as amended)

Between

PROFESSOR ALEXANDER MONIZ ("Claimant")

Vs.

PROFESSOR CINDY STEWART ("Respondent")

FINAL AWARD

Appearances:

For the Claimant: Professor Alexander Moniz;
BTh., M.A., B.A.

For the Respondent: Professor Cindy Stewart;
PhD., M.A., B.A.

Arbitrator: William Hansen
Hearing Date: September 17, 2014
Hearing Location: McMaster University, Hamilton
Ontario, Canada

Decision: January 14, 2015

Statement of Claim

That both God and Jesus are real. That Jesus spent time on earth as a human. That Jesus is the manifest son of the God of Abraham as described in the Holy Bible.

Role of the Arbitrator under the *Agreement for Arbitration*:

As provided for under the *Agreement for Arbitration* the Arbitrator can make a finding to:

- Support the Claimant's position and find Jesus is the son of God.
- Both God and Jesus are real.
- Dismiss the Claim for lack of evidence.

In addition the Arbitrator may determine:

- Specific claims have a factual basis, in whole or in part.

FINAL AWARD

The Claimant and Respondent have given me the responsibility and authority to decide their dispute, under the Arbitration Act of Ontario, (Revised Statutes) that has been amended, and in effect as of the date(s) in which this arbitration hearing is conducted.

Eligibility:

The parties represented in this matter did not question the eligibility or qualifications of either of the proponents as being capable and knowledgeable to present their respective positions. The arbitration proceeded under the terms agreed upon by the parties.

Introduction:

The parties were informed of the arbitration process, its procedure, governing law, the Agreement for Arbitration, the role and responsibilities of the parties, the Arbitrator, and the purpose of the hearing. All witnesses either affirmed the truthfulness of their testimony or took an oath on the Holy Bible.

Preliminary Issues:

The Claimant and the Respondent did not ask me to decide any preliminary questions.

The Standard Used to Determine the Question:

By mutual consent the parties agreed that the Claimant is the proponent, and as such will have the onus to prove any claims being made. The Respondent will respond and challenge said claims.

In order for the Claimant's position to succeed, the evidence and testimony must satisfy me that their case is sufficient to find that Jesus and God exist and that Jesus is the son of God.

What is the standard that I am required to use as a measurement? Unlike some proceedings, the highest test is known as *"beyond all doubt."* Such onus on any Claimant is considered, by most civilized jurisdictions, to be totally unreasonable and is never applied.

The second standard used to make a determination is known as *"beyond a reasonable doubt."*

This has been used for a very long time and is a part of our history and traditions of justice. It is so engrained in criminal law that some think it needs no explanation, yet something must be said regarding its meaning.

A reasonable doubt is not an imaginary or frivolous doubt. It must not be based upon sympathy or prejudice. Rather, it is based on reason and common sense. It is logically derived from the evidence or absence of evidence.

A proposition, beyond a reasonable doubt, would seem to be fair in this arbitration. However, I find that due to the historical debate on this matter this is a rather high standard of proof. In these circumstances I have given the benefit to the Claimant. All must remember that it is virtually impossible to prove anything to an absolute certainty and even to prove something beyond a reasonable doubt is extremely high.

Some may argue that claiming such a proposition, as in this matter, should be a high standard, as extraordinary claims should produce extraordinary evidence. In short, arbitration has a much lower standard than that of a reasonable doubt.

A third standard of evidence is known as *"a preponderance of evidence."* This preponderance is based on the more convincing evidence and its probable truth or accuracy, and not on the amount of evidence. Thus, one clearly knowledgeable witness may provide a preponderance of evidence over a dozen witnesses with hazy testimony, or a signed agreement with definite terms may outweigh opinions or speculation about what the parties intended.

Preponderance of evidence is contrasted with **"beyond a reasonable doub***t***,"** which is the more severe test of evidence required. No matter what the definition stated in various standards, all standards are somewhat subjective.

The last and lowest standard of proof is known as *"the balance of probabilities"*. The balance of probability standard means that an arbitrator is satisfied an event occurred, or a proposition is true, if the arbitrator considers that, on the evidence, the occurrence of the event or the proposition was more likely than not.

When assessing the probabilities, the arbitrator will have in mind, as a factor, to whatever extent is appropriate in the particular case, that the more serious the allegation the less likely it is that the event occurred and, hence, the stronger should be the evidence before the arbitrator concludes that the allegation is established on the balance of probability.

Example: A claim that a person was raised from the dead, would require substantial and stronger evidence, but a claim that a person was stoned to death, in an era when stoning was commonplace, may not require as much convincing evidence.

Built into the probability standard is a generous degree of flexibility in respect of the seriousness of the allegation. Although the result is much the same, this does not mean that where a serious allegation is in issue, the standard of proof required is higher. It means only that the inherent probability or improbability of an event is itself a matter to be taken into account when weighing the probabilities and deciding whether, on balance, the event occurred or the proposition is true.

The more improbable the claim, the stronger must be the evidence. The party, trying to prove a fact, has to establish that it is more probable than not that the fact is true, thus tipping the scales sufficiently to convince one to accept one fact or set of facts over another. In other words, the Claimant must just tip the scales in favour of the position put forth.

This is the lowest standard of proof in most proceedings. This is the standard applied in this matter and the test in which the Claimant must meet.

Background and Question(s) to Decide:

The **Claimant** asserts there is a god. That God sent his son to earth in human form. That God's son was named Jesus and the events surrounding the life of Jesus are chronicled and documented in the Holy Bible. The Claimant submits the Bible is a historical record of the actions, decrees and commandments of God and proof of the life, death and resurrection of Jesus Christ, son of God.

The **Respondent** claims the evidence to support the Claimant's proposition is insufficient, hearsay, and contradictory. The Respondent claim the author or authors of the Bible are not identified, no original manuscripts of the Bible exists, and among other claims, there is no independent or corroborated testimony or historical records to support that a Jesus, as chronicled, in the Bible ever existed. The Respondent states the Claimant is unable to produce the minimum standards of evidence to even come close to meet the balance of probabilities.

Agreed Upon Facts:

- The Holy Bible is the recognized book of the Christian faith.

- Millions of copies of the Bible have been reproduced in most languages of the world.

- For the purposes of this hearing, the King James Version of the Bible will be the main reference and deciding document when matters of fact, testimony or evidence are in dispute.

- There appears to be no dispute between the parties that a book, usually described as the Bible, does exist. There appears to be no dispute that millions of people believe the Bible is the word of God.

Facts, Evidence and Argument:

The Bible – Claimant's Position

The Claimant argued in greater detail, but I have for brevity summarized the Claimant's position. The Claimant's main source of reference is the King James version of the Holy Bible. Each party was restricted to calling no more than five experts to testify on their behalf. Such experts could be re-called to testify in multiple disciplines, if so qualified. The Claimant argued the following:

- The Bible is the best historical document that supports both the existence of God and his son Jesus.

- Five experts in the fields of theology, history, archaeology, linguistics and comparative literature, testified and presented evidence that supported the Claimant's position.

- The Claimant made reference to over 25,000 hand-written manuscripts in Greek, Latin and Hebrew, among other languages that suggest the word of God is written into the Bible as we know it.

- The Claimant's expert in the historicity of the Bible testified that historical biblical events were not recorded along a single lineal line, but rather many individual events occurred at various times and places that required them to be stitched together, much as a jig-saw puzzle, when and if missing pieces were discovered. He claimed that verification of biblical events is still being found, such as the Dead Sea Scrolls and other archaeological finds.

- The Claimant summarized the expert testimony by clarifying that the Bible is not written in which a history book would be written today, as the Bible is more than a historical record of biblical events. The message in the Bible is about God's promise and mankind's relationship with each other and the heavenly father through Christ.

- The authors of the Bible did not intend it to be strictly historical; but rather historically determined expressions of our relationship to God. It was written in a form that was typical of the time.

- The truth lies not in an absolute commitment to facts, nor a detailed recording of history, but rather the ability of man, 2,000 years ago, to express the reality the way it was experienced in those days.

The Bible – Respondent's Position

- The Respondent challenged the historical references made in the Bible as total fiction, or at best, an exaggerated account of mythical events that were embellished over time by those wanting to establish another god to praise in the name of a particular religion.

- The Respondent brought to the witness stand experts with equally high qualifications in their field of study. All the experts testified that it is virtually impossible to verify the claims made in the Bible as there is no independent record of any of the astounding biblical claims or events. The experts, in meticulous detail, explained how events witnessed by thousands, such as the Sermon on the Mount, the parting of the Red Sea, the Tower of Babel (to explain diversity of languages), raising of the dead, resurrection of Christ, holding the Sun in place for twenty-four hours, feeding thousands with a few loaves of bread and a few fishes is far from meeting the test of probability, but is impossible to have occurred. In addition there is no verifiable historical record that any of these miraculous events ever happened.

- The Respondent argued, according to most historians; if the parting of the Red Sea by Moses did occur as recorded in the Bible, (con't)

- it was witnessed by millions of people. Such a supernatural event would have most assuredly been recorded in the history writings of the time. No such reliable evidence or records exist, other than the Bible.

- The Respondent submitted that any one of these events would have been so astounding that it would have created such a commotion among the population that historical records, independent of the Bible, would have flourished on stone tablets, animal hides, clay tablets, parchment, as well as various ornaments, carvings, statues and symbols. Yet there is absolutely no verifiable record. Logic, reason and common sense would demand there be thousands of historical records. There is none. No proof.

- According to the Respondent, the most fallacious of all arguments is the claim that the earth is only 6,000 years old and everything was created in seven days. The Respondent provided evidence that all of the above defy astronomy, palaeontology, archaeology, biology, chemistry, geology, climatology, all the laws of physics; and most assuredly, most human behavioural sciences.

- The Respondent disputed the efficacy of hand written manuscripts, as none were originals, that could be traced to verify biblical writings. Most of the manuscripts entered into evidence were either re-written several times over the ages, re-interpreted into languages which changed their original meaning, and often words were added or deleted and not one of the authors were absolutely known to exist.

- All of the above was given into testimony by the Respondent's expert witnesses. All of the evidence and testimony is *"hearsay"*. The Respondent reminded the hearing that *"hearsay"* is generally inadmissible as evidence because it is based on the reports of others rather than on the personal knowledge of a witness.

- The Respondents' experts testified that the physical evidence of a living Christ or a God of Abraham is sketchy at best and in most respects, non-existent. Studies of manuscripts, and the Dead Sea Scrolls, say virtually nothing about Jesus, but a lot about the Jewish religion and the in-fighting among sects. The scrolls and manuscripts are evidence of growing religious dogma that was an outgrowth of previously held mythical gods and fabricated stories. The Respondent submitted evidence that most experts (including those who testified for the Claimant) agree the Dead Sea Scrolls was written during the period from 520 B.C.E.-70 C.E. The Respondent claimed this includes a period over the entire lifespan of Jesus; yet not a mention of the miracles or the incredible achievements of Jesus.

Millions of People Believe in God –Claimant's Position

- The Claimant argued that it would be impossible for millions of people to believe in God if he did not exist. The Claimant produced an impressive list of the names of well-known scholars, physicians, scientists, presidents and world leaders, and a host of highly educated and respected citizens who believe in God and Jesus Christ as the son of God.

- The Claimant argued many respected governments around the world acknowledges God's existence. In the United States of America the words *"In God We Trust"* appears on their currency. Any responsible government would never put their trust in something that doesn't exist. The evidence is clear that God exists and an overwhelming number of people believe it to be true.

Believe in God – Respondent's Position

- The Respondent agreed with the Claimant that millions of people believe that God exists. The Respondent produced evidence and expert testimony that many millions of people believe in a god, just not the Christian god being argued by the Claimant. The Respondent produced evidence that suggested 1/3 of the world's population is composed of numerous Christian religions that believe in the Claimant's god. However 2/3 of the world's population believes in a variety of other gods or no god at all. The Respondent produced additional evidence and expert testimony that demonstrated throughout the history of mankind many thousands of gods and religions have come and gone. Some of these religions, like Christianity and Islam have been more successful than others in proselytizing their religion and their god.

- The Respondent submitted evidence that millions of people used to believe that the sun revolved around the earth, a position once held by the very religion supported by the Claimant. People believed that the earth was flat, blood-letting cured illnesses, witches existed, there is life after death, (con't)

- and despite the evidence; and/or lack of evidence that any of this is true, there are still today millions of people who believe one or more of the above. The Respondent submitted additional evidence, by way of documents and expert corroboration that belief in anything, by millions of people, is not proof that their belief is based upon fact or reality. In other words people, over the history of mankind, people believed in many different things that never existed or were proven later to be false.

- The Respondent produced an impressive history of the reasons for the *"In God We Trust"* motto on American currency. In essence the Respondent claimed there were both religious and political motivations behind this act. The Respondent posed a question; *"Have governments ever been wrong?"* The Respondent also quoted the following Bible passage when the following was attributed to Jesus:

Matthew 6:24 *"You can't worship two gods at once. Loving one god, you'll end up hating the other. Adoration of one feeds contempt for the other. You can't worship God and Money both."*

The Respondent suggested that if there was a God, he would take a very dim view of how a people would debase his name by placing it on their money.

The Claimant completed his presentation of the evidence and testimony and the Respondent presented her case.

Where is God? – The Respondent's Position

- The Respondent submitted studies indicating there is no god.

- Two experts testified in support of their 50 years of research that supports the position of a godless universe. The Respondent claimed you cannot see, hear, feel, taste or smell anything that represents a god.

- Since the Respondent raised this issue, and called expert witnesses to support her claim, the Claimant was allowed to call an expert theologian to testify on this matter.

- The Claimant's witness testified, under oath, that he regularly speaks to God through prayer. The witness was asked a number of questions as to whether God replies, answers prayers, is God visible, does God speak to the witness; and several other questions regarding the physical attributes of God. The Claimant's witness, under examination, explained God in the following manner:

- The human and physical world is incapable of understanding God unless they accept Jesus Christ as their saviour. God is above the world, and his involvement in the world, are transcendent and all pervasive. God is therefore eternal and infinite, not controlled by the created world and beyond human events. Any philosophical discussion is inept in understanding the metaphysical theories of divine presence in which the divine encompasses or is manifested in the material world. The transcendent nature of God is a reality beyond what is perceptible to the senses. God is involved in the world by Christian teachings by way of his message through his son Jesus Christ. Those who do not accept God's word through Christ (con't) cannot understand the existence of God the Creator of all that is, ever was, and ever will be.

- The following exchange between the Respondent and the Claimant's witness may help to clarify this discussion.

Respondent: Are you saying we must just accept on faith that there is a God?

Witness: Yes, but first you must accept Jesus to have faith.

Respondent: What exactly do you mean accept Jesus?

Witness: God sent Jesus to spread the word as it is written in the Bible.

Respondent: Who wrote the Bible?

Witness: Prophets, scribes, and priests who witnessed the works of Jesus or who heard the word of God.

Respondent: How do you know this?

Witness: It is written in the Bible.

Respondent: But you don't know who wrote the Bible?

Witness: I just told you who wrote the Bible.

Respondent: Do any of these folks, who wrote the Bible, have names, or can you provide evidence of who they were?

Witness: I don't know their names, except for the evidence that David wrote most of the Psalms and Paul wrote much of the New Testament.

Respondent: How do you know this?

Witness: By reading the Bible.

Respondent: If I gave you the book *"Alice in Wonderland"*, would you believe the exploits of Alice?

Witness: Of course not, that book is a fairy tale.

Respondent: How do you know the stories in the Bible, like Noah's Ark, the Tower of Babel, the parting of the Red Sea, Jonah and the Whale, David and Goliath, Daniel in the Lion's Den are not all fairy tales?

Witness: They are not fairy tales.

Respondent: Why do you say that?

Witness: Because the word of God is not fairy tales.

Respondent: How do you know this is the word of God?

Witness: Because it is written in the Bible.

Respondent: What happens to all the people who do not believe in your God or accept Jesus?

Witness: They are condemned to an eternity in hell.

Respondent: Do you mean people like Mahatma Gandhi, the Dalai Llama, Gautama Buddha, (con't)

Nelson Mandela and Malala Yousafzai are all condemned to spend eternity in hell?

Witness: Yes, if they have not accepted Jesus and are not Christians.

Respondent: If some serial killer, on his deathbed, confesses all his sins, accepts Jesus and converts to Christianity, will he go to heaven?

Witness: If he is sincere, the answer is 'yes'.

Respondent: I have no more use of this witness.

Bible's Contradictions, Inaccuracies, Fallacies and Impossibilities – Respondent

Over a five day period, the Respondent, under expert testimony, examined 150 errant passages in the Bible and assertions made by the Claimant. For purposes of brevity just three examples are provided.

The Respondent's witness stated some contradictions are most unusual as it appears in different Chapters of the same book. In John the contradiction, suggests this book was written by different authors; either that or Jesus forgets what he said, or has no idea what he said previously.

John 10:30 *"I and my Father are one."*

John 14:28 *"Ye have heard how I said unto you, I go away, and come again unto you. If ye loved me, ye would rejoice, because I said, I go unto the Father: For my Father is greater than I."*

Once again in the book of Acts we have two different versions of the same episode during Paul's journey to Damascus. The writer(s) cannot seem to get their stories straight as to what they heard or saw.

ACT 9:7 *"And the men which journeyed with him stood speechless, <u>hearing a voice,</u> but seeing no man."*

ACT 22:9 *"And they that were with me saw indeed the light, and were afraid; <u>but they heard not the voice</u> of him that spake to me."*

In one short sentence God spoke and said in **Isaiah 45:7**; *"I make peace and create evil,"* A contradiction in one sentence.

The Claimant did not call a witness to refute claims made by the Respondent and indicated he would respond to these claims in his summation.

Summation – Claimant

The Claimant stated that religion was a matter of doing God's work rather than thinking about what God is or is not. Christian faith understands that others will frequently misrepresent the tradition and message of Christ. Much of the Bible was not intended to be understood literally because it was only possible to speak about a reality that transcended language in symbolic terms. The story of Christ, in the Bible, was written as a message of how to live and treat others. It was never intended to be a factual account of historical events.

God's message, through Jesus Christ had its purpose to help us to contemplate the human predicament.

And face the challenges of life in a spiritual manner. The story of creation was emphatically not intended as a literal account of the physical origins of life and if biblical text appeared to contradict current scientific discoveries, the scholars must interpret it differently. The Bible is the word of God, interpreted through fallible man. Unfortunately people are not perfect, unlike God, and people forget, or see things differently. Sure there are contradictions in the Bible, but life is a contradiction. Five people could see something from five different perspectives and are likely to get the specific details a little different. This is to be expected. It is only human

The problem arises when mere humans attempt to interpret theology. They have a mind-set that blocks their understanding as they are not enlightened.

They live in a world of a physical presence and are incapable of understanding faith-based reality. God is a concept of sensory perception that is comparable to awareness without the natural elements of human weaknesses. God's mind is free from the constant influx of thought. God appears in a special awareness when expressed through the lens of human consciousness.

Religion was never supposed to provide answers to questions that lay within the reach of human reason. Religion's task is to help us to live creatively, peacefully, and even joyously with the realities of life for which there were no easy answers. Religion and the message of God, through Jesus Christ, help to provide the explanations to the problems of morality, pain, grief, despair, and outrage at the injustice and cruelty of life.

It is also wrong to suggest that God is subject to scientific hypothesis, study or analysis.

God is a belief for bringing transparency and understanding to the human race that is not subject to a series of experiments and observations. God is not material, so you cannot see, hear, smell or taste him. Those who cannot grasp this concept will never be able to understand the properties, purpose and reality of God.

Summation – Respondent

We all live in a real world, not an imaginary one. The evidence and testimony from the expert witnesses, on both sides of this question, confirmed that the Bible is full of fallacies, inaccuracies and contradictions.

The Claimant relies heavily on the King James Version of the Holy Bible as proof of a god, and of a man named Jesus, and at the same time acknowledging the Bible's inconsistencies; then proceeds to tell this hearing that the Bible was not written as a historical record of events.

The Claimant states very clearly that the Bible is a historical record of God and Jesus. In the very next breath the Claimant's own expert witnesses testify that the Bible was not written as an historical record of biblical events. The Claimant can not have it both ways. The Bible is a historical record of the activities of God and Jesus or it is not; it can't be both.

The Claimant argues that historical details that differ in the Bible are the result of human error, not due to God's message. This answer is lame. One is compelled to ask; *"Why would this perfect, special form of perfect being entrust his fallible human creations with his divine message?"* All answers to this question defy logic. The Claimant states as mere humans, who have not accepted Christ, cannot understand *'faith-based reality'*.

The term itself *'faith-based reality'*, is a contradiction in terms. *'faith'* is belief without evidence. *'Reality'* is a proven truth, with evidence. Once again the Claimant is suffering from a form of delusion known as cognitive dissonance by attempting to hold contradictory statements that are clearly in conflict.

The Respondent submitted that the evidence of the <u>non-existence</u> of any god, and Jesus, is proven, not only on the balance of probabilities, but beyond any reasonable doubt. The Respondent maintains the Bible is contradictory, contains many errors of fact, is fallacious in the extreme, has no independent source of corroboration, especially when claiming miracles that astounds the human race even today.

The Claimant's case relies solely on hearsay; there is no evidence of who the actual authors are, the evidence shows that the Bible was copied, re-written and modified many times over by different people, and the final absurdity of all, is the clam that this all-perfect god would permit such an imperfect book to be his word for the very subjects that he created. This hearing is expected to believe that any normal, clear-thinking human being, is supposed to accept this premise.

In addressing the claim that so many people believe in God, the Respondent in her summation outlined her position. The Respondent presented a thorough examination of submissions and evidence supported by expert witnesses, during the hearing that the human race had since its known beginnings, praised and believed in many thousands of different gods. The Respondent went on to say that it is a fact that millions of people today believe in their own special god.

For any one religion to lay claim to their god, as the one and only god, is yet another fallacious argument. How could it be that only their god is the real true god? If there is only a single god, then all the many other religions are wrong. If there is only the Christian god, then which branch of the Christian religion is correct? There are many thousand different Christian religions that dispute each others interpretation of the Bible. All of these Christian religions hold various rituals, or have special rules to follow. All through history Christians have killed one another in proclaiming their Christian sect was the right one. Which brand of Christian belief is the one true religion?

For Christians to believe, that the creator of the world and the universe would bring his message only to a tiny fraction of the world in the Middle East is preposterous.

It is beyond all comprehension. Why were the rest of the peoples' of the world ignored? Why would the creator of everything pay no attention to the rest of Africa, Asia, Australia, North and South America and most of what is today Europe?

Why would not this same God speak to the millions of people in China, India and the various indigenous peoples around the world? Did they have their own gods or no god at all to speak to them?

The answer is obvious. The current gods that are being praised and hallowed are no different than the many gods that have preceded them. The only real difference is that some religions, like Christianity, have been able to convince many uninformed and desperate people to believe in a supernatural power beyond the reality of nature, science, and logical reasoning.

The Respondent concluded her summation by saying that the evidence, physical, historical, and through expert analysis and study, is compelling and persuasive, in the extreme, that demonstrates there is no god and no Jesus, as portrayed in the Bible. The entire story was fabricated for religious purposes as a way to manipulate people to believe in a supernatural power. The Respondent submitted that God did not create man, but man created many gods in the name of their special type of religion.

Findings:

At the outset of the hearing the parties agreed to various terms and parameters in which this arbitration would be conducted. For instance the amount of printed material, documents, books, and reference mater etc. was restricted.

Each party was limited to calling only five expert witnesses in their respective chosen field of expertise; although witnesses could be recalled a second or third time to elabourate further on points of examination or cross-examination.

In total the hearing took place over a three-month period or 480 hours of testimony, and resulted in a transcript of 45,000 pages of the proceedings.

This question of the existence of God, or a god, has confounded human civilization since the beginning of time. Regardless of the decision in this matter, I do not expect that the debate over this question will be resolved - at least not in my lifetime. I find in this matter, unlike most arbitration decisions; the final award will not be final as the debate will continue. However a finding as to the claim being made is my responsibility and mandate. The following is my finding.

This hearing is compelled to assess the evidence and testimony of the parties based upon the facts and the balance of probabilities, that God and Jesus, does or did exist, and both are real.

The operative word in the above sentence is 'real'. The word real means, genuine, existent, actual or true. The evidence and testimony in this case persuades me that all of us, believers and non-believers in a god or deity, live in the physical and natural world we call earth. This is a fact. I therefore find this is real.

Others who live in this real world also believe there is another world; a world they call heaven. These folks believe in a god and accept the Bible as the word of God.

It is as though we all live together on this world, but travel on parallel tracks, side by side. While on this earth we work, play and spend our life together, until we, as individuals, meet the end of the track. Some believe that the end of the track is the end of life. Others believe that at the end of their track they move on to the after-life. Proof of who is correct has not been provided and perhaps, never will.

I find that the physical evidence provided by the Respondent to be compelling, persuasive and to stand scrutiny under questioning. I find that the evidence and testimony from the Claimant to lack corroboration, and the witnesses for the Claimant were not able to adequately support their positions with verification of the historical documents or references in which they relied upon.

However my decision is not based upon this finding alone. The hearing is left with other matters to consider with respect to the claim being made.

People believe in many things for different reasons and this includes the belief in a god.

Competing Belief Systems

All humans have their own belief system, and it is our way to cope and deal with a confusing world. Some ascribe to the evidence-based system, others the faith-based system.

Science, reality and reason is used to build an evidence-based belief system. The key element of science is the need to test, verify, examine, replicate and prove, beyond all reasonable likelihood that something is true, based upon the evidence available at any given time. It also recognizes that humans possess individual beliefs, and consequently are capable of introducing bias in their interpretation of the world.

Science attempts to mitigate against such bias by requiring strict definitions of terms and conditions, as well as demanding that any evidence be capable of independent verification by others. This ensures that accepted results have been subjected to trials that may also be subject to bias, by following a strict adherence to procedure, such biases will cancel each other out and conclusions are largely objective.

Faith-based belief systems are mental constructs that do not require conclusive evidence. Does this diminish their value? It is this point of departure between the two systems that help to define an important difference. In short, a faith-based belief system is unequivocally based on the lack of evidence or evidence which may be impossible to collect.

Some consider faith-based beliefs as less valuable or a construct of their imagination. We draw these conclusions, because regardless of what we individually believe, we are all convinced that our particular beliefs are the correct ones. It is this tug-of-war of which is right and which is wrong that is the cause of tension between the two positions. We will defend our particular belief systems vigorously as being the only means by which one can experience truth or reality.

However, it is important to note that not all beliefs are subject to verification and this is where these two forms of beliefs often collide.

One cannot introduce faith into an evidence-based system any more than one can demand evidence of a faith-based system.

Faith-based belief systems are subject to interpretation. Strongly held beliefs or opinions are never changed except by consensus. If enough individuals agree, then a particular tenet of a belief may become so rigid that a mountain of evidence is totally useless in any attempt to change minds.

A strongly held religious belief that poisonous snake bites will not harm true believers is so emotionally entrenched in their conviction that it is pointless to argue otherwise. The same emotional commitment is at work with those who believe in an after-life. To challenge such religious beliefs with reason becomes a fruitless exercise because there is never any evidence for the faith-based believer to consider.

People seem to need something to believe in to give lives meaning and purpose. Each of us has our own sense of reality.

Believers have a difficult time in accepting that we are all here by some kind of mistake. Believers can not tolerate the idea that the world operates according to no particular rules. Concepts like randomness; is rejected by believers. They are inclined to dismiss any idea that suggests that there is no purpose or meaning to life. They subvert most scientific explanations and resort to a belief in a deity that is the source of all meaning.

When science ventures into areas where such ideas dominate, they attempt to analyze what is currently available to address the most contested topics. It isn't that scientists are better equipped to deal with uncertainty; it's just that scientists have collected more evidence and data, which allows them to make sense of the randomness. The world still has purpose and meaning. It is simply different, depending upon your perspective and beliefs.

Faith-based beliefs seem to have no explanation for all of the bad that happens in our world. They suggest bad things are the work of the devil or some evil source. Whenever good occurs, or what appears to be a miracle, they claim it is the work of God. In either case, believers want to presume that events have a purpose and that they have been executed by someone or something with intent, even if they don't always understand what that intent might be.

Evidence-based belief systems suggest that things happen in this world for no good or bad reason. In the case of the natural world; if lightning were to strike a toddler riding his tricycle, it was neither the devil nor a god that sent the deadly bolt of lightning. Nature is indifferent. It is random. The world isn't intrinsically hostile, or intrinsically safe. It doesn't care and it doesn't play favourites.

So, we construct our respective belief systems so that we can tell the stories that make us feel most comfortable. In that world, everything always has a reason.

I thought the foregoing was important so that my decision is put into some kind of context.

I find, that based upon the enormous amount of evidence, the testimony of several highly regarded scholars, researchers, historians and many other experts in the areas respecting the matter under consideration; that based upon the balance of probabilities, it is more probable than not, that the God and the stories in the Bible are a construct of man's superstition, that has a historical record of human behaviour in almost all human societies since mankind started to question the unexplained.

My finding of the above is based upon the evidence available and presented during this hearing. This finding does not suggest, for the millions of people who believe in a god, that they are wrong. For who, what person can be the paragon of all knowledge? There is no such person or indeed such people.

If we, as civilized people, are to co-exist; no: more than co-exist, but rather live in harmony as we travel together along the parallel tracks of life, we must respect each others right to hold competing beliefs. If our beliefs become the reason for our eventual destruction, than we have failed to live up to any measure of morality and ethics.

My finding is one that I hold today. Perhaps, as so much has changed in human history, this too may change at a future time - in another forum. Before I dismiss the parties, there will no doubt be a frenzy of media questions.

The media will attempt to bait you to engage in acrimony and disparage the other. I suggest you not take the bait. I also suggest that you reflect upon what we have done here over the past three months? If anyone or anything won in this matter it was the profound significance that helped to further an understanding and shed additional light on a subject that is fundamental to the human condition. It will serve no purpose to crow or denigrate.

Conclusion and Ruling:

To conclude that God and/or Jesus are not real depends with whom you are talking. Many millions of people believe God is real. No amount of evidence, at this hearing, will change this fact. Facts and evidence alone, for some, is not a basis for their belief.

I conclude that people will believe for reasons they hold true, regardless of any suggestion to the contrary. In this; the world of physics, biology, natural science, verifiable recorded history, and my current understanding of how the world and life began; I find that based upon the evidence provided, at this time, during this hearing, that on the balance of probabilities, it is more probable than not, that there is no God and the person as described in the Bible as Jesus, was an elabourate fabrication by man.

The claim that God is real is dismissed for lack of evidence. This is my ruling on the matter before me.

Dated this 14th. Day of January, 2015.

William Hansen - Arbitrator

~

Resources and Other Things for Atheists/Humanists and Thoughtful Religionists

Meet-ups

"Let us tenderly and kindly cherish, therefore, the means of knowledge. Let us dare to read, think speak and write."
—John Adams

Facepalm

"For all you kids watching at home, Santa just is white. Just because it makes you uncomfortable doesn't mean it has to change. Jesus was a white man, too."
—Megyn Kelly (Fox News)

"It is a just retribution for improper sexual misconduct."
—Mother Teresa, on AIDS

"Evolution is a bankrupt speculative philosophy, not a scientific fact. Only a spiritually bankrupt society could ever believe it.... Only atheists could accept this Satanic theory."   **—Jimmy Swaggart**

"To assert that the earth revolves around the sun is as erroneous as to claim that Jesus was not born of a virgin."
—Cardinal Bellarmine, 1615, during the trial of Galileo

Facepalm

From the Bible:

Question: Why do snakes have no legs or feet?
Answer: Because Eve ate fruit. Genesis 3:13–14

Question: What is marriage?
Answer: Marriage is a union between one man and one….or more…women.
Genesis 4:19, 16:3, 21:1–13, 25:6, 26:34, 29:17–28, Exodus 2:15–21, II Samuel 3:2–5.

Note: There are too many other mentions in the Bible regarding polygamy, but one cannot ignore the most famous Bible polygamist of them all. This is found in I Kings chapter 11:1–3, which states: ***"But King Solomon loved many strange women, together with the daughter of Pharaoh, women of the Moabites, Ammonites, Edomites, Zidonians, and Hittites; Of the nations concerning which the LORD said unto the children of Israel, Ye shall not go in to them, neither shall they come in unto you: for surely they will turn away your heart after their gods: Solomon clave unto these in love. And he had seven hundred wives, princesses, and three hundred concubines: and his wives turned away his heart."***

However, God was not happy with Solomon's conduct, not because of polygamy, but because Solomon and his women were praising other gods. ***"And the LORD was angry with Solomon, because his heart was turned from the LORD God of Israel, which had appeared unto him twice, and had commanded him concerning this thing, that he should not go after other gods: but he kept not that which the LORD commanded."***

Question: What is the penalty for picking up sticks on the Sabbath?

Answer: Death. (Numbers 15:32–36)

"And while the children of Israel were in the wilderness, they found a man that gathered sticks upon the Sabbath day. And they that found him gathering sticks brought him unto Moses and Aaron, and unto all the congregation. And they put him in ward, because it was not declared what should be done to him. And the LORD said unto Moses, The man shall be surely put to death: all the congregation shall stone him with stones without the camp. And all the congregation brought him without the camp, and stoned him with stones, and he died; as the LORD commanded Moses."

Oh my, holy crackers! And this is the loving, forgiving, generous god? Well here is one Christian response: *"The majority of these instances are examples to the community so that the people would take God seriously when he gives them commands."* Go figure.

Question: What does the Bible say about sex?

Answer: There is no way this can be kept brief; you would need to read the entire Bible. However a reading of Leviticus, Chapter 20, will give you some idea. Here is a sampling.

- *"If a man commits adultery with another man's wife — with the wife of his neighbour — both the adulterer and the adulteress are to be put to death."* (Well, that's one way to keep the population explosion in check.)

- *"If a man has sexual relations with his father's wife* [wouldn't this be his mother or mother-in-law?] *he has dishonoured his father. Both the man and the woman are to be put to death; their blood will be on their own heads."*

- *"If a man has sexual relations with a man as one does with a woman, both of them have done what is detestable. They are to be put to death; their blood will be on their own heads."* (And this is the loving god?)

- *"If a man marries both a woman and her mother, it is wicked. Both he and they must be burned in the fire, so that no wickedness will be among you."* (This helps to explain rules of polygamy. I wonder why in this case it is death by fire.)

- *"If a man has sexual relations with an animal, he is to be put to death, and you must kill the animal."* (Why kill the poor animal? I'm sure it wasn't consensual sex.)

- *"If a man marries his brother's wife, it is an act of impurity; he has dishonoured his brother. They will be childless."* (Talk about confusing messages; see Genesis 38:8–10.)

- *"And Judah said unto Onan, Go in unto thy brother's wife, and marry her, and raise up seed to thy brother. And Onan knew that the seed should not be his; and it came to pass, when he went in unto his brother's wife, that he spilled it on the ground, lest that he should give seed to his brother."*

(Now listen up, here. What did God do to Onan for not impregnating his brother's wife? God inflicted his usual punishment; he killed him. Go figure.)

Enough of this Old Testament stuff. Do you remember what Jesus said about all this? In his famous Sermon on the Mount in Matthew 5:17, he said he came to fulfill these laws. He even went further in Matthew 5:28. He said don't even look at another woman and think about having sex with her; if you do, you have already committed adultery. Then in Matthew 5:32, he says if you marry a divorced woman both of you have committed adultery. I wonder how many divorced religious sinners out there are following the teachings of Jesus?

This is enough facepalm from the Bible. What, you say? The entire Bible is facepalm.

From the Believers:

A devout Christian speaking on a PBS documentary on religion said the following: *"If the Bible said 2 + 2 = 5, then I would believe it."* Nobody should be surprised here, after all, the Catholics do claim that 1 God + 1 Jesus + 1 Holy Ghost = 1. Therefore, $1 + 1 + 1 = 1$.

"Sometimes I wish God would give me a Holy Ghost machine gun. I'd blow your head off!" —**Benny Hinn**

"God help anyone who would try to get in a way of TBN, which was God's plan. I have attended the funeral of at least two people who tried." —**Paul Crouch** (TBN is the Trinity Broadcasting Network)

"There is something wrong if a Christian doesn't become rich." —**Kenneth Copeland**

"God said: 'it is time to tell the money you don't belong to the wicked, you belong to us.'... Money come to me now!" —**Leroy Thompson**

"Pregnancy from rape is a gift that God intended."
—**Republican Senate candidate, Richard Mourdock**

"I once asked the Lord why so many people are confused and he said to me, 'Tell them to stop trying to figure everything out, and they will stop being confused,' I found it to be absolutely true. Reasoning and confusion go together."
—**Joyce Meyer, *Battlefield of the Mind for Teens***

It's time to stomp out atheists in America. The majority of Americans would love to see atheists kicked out of America. If you don't believe in god, then get out of this country.

The United States of America is based upon having freedom of religion, speech etc., which means you can believe in God anyway you want (Baptist, Catholic, Methodist, etc.), but you must believe. I don't recall freedom of religion meaning no religion. Our currency even says, "In God We Trust." So to all the atheists in America: Get off of our country.

Atheists have caused the ruin of this great nation by taking prayer out of our schools and being able to practice what can only be called evil. I don't care if they have never committed a crime; atheists are the reason crime is rampant.

—A Letter to the Editor – American Newspaper

"When the temptation to masturbate is strong, yell 'Stop!' to those thoughts as loudly as you can in your mind. Then recite a portion of the Bible or sing a hymn."
—Mormon Guide to Self-Control

"Sex education classes in our public schools are promoting incest." **—Jimmy Swaggart**

A Word or Two from Others:

"No, I don't know that atheists should be considered as citizens, nor should they be considered patriots. This is one nation under God."
—George Herbert Walker Bush, Former U.S. President, 1988

"We don't have to protect the environment; the Second Coming is at hand."
—James Watt, Secretary of the Interior during the Regan years

"We're going to bring back God and the Bible and drive the gods of secular humanism right out of the public schools of America."
—Presidential candidate Pat Buchanan addressing the anti-gay rally in Des Moines, 2-11-96

"[T]his monkey mythology of Darwin is the cause of permissiveness, promiscuity, prophylactics, perversions, pregnancies, abortions, pornotherapy, pollution, poisoning and proliferation of crimes of all types."
—Judge Braswell Dean, in *Time* magazine, March 1981

This final quote is from an anonymous source. Am I glad that I got this one clarified. This was one thing that always bothered me. Now I know the answer.

"It is true that we all descended from Adam and Eve, but the 'fact' that Eve was black is a myth. No one knows about her color but she was made from Adam's rib and all ribs are white."

—Anonymous

~

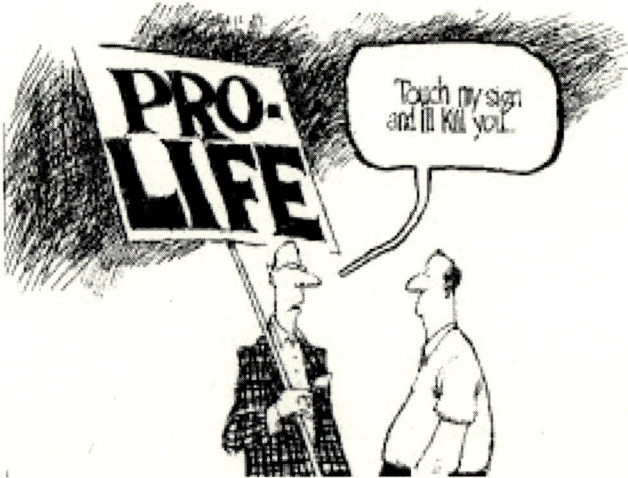

Religious Rules and Beliefs

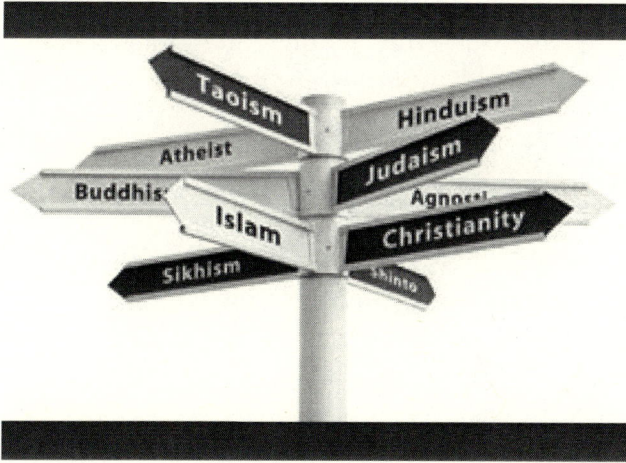

"*If a man would follow, today, the teachings of the Old Testament, he would be a criminal. If he would follow strictly the teachings of the New Testament, he would be insane.*"

—Robert G. Ingersoll

Religious Rules and Beliefs

An atheist could make all kinds of negative commentary on these various religious rules and beliefs. While the temptation is great, there are times when no comment is necessary. This is a list of 100 religious rules and beliefs. There are many more. I have not identified the various religions that subscribe to these rules and beliefs. The reader will be able to identify some of these religions. See how many you can identify.

What terrifies me are the billions of people who actually follow these rules or believe this nonsense.

1. **Which hand to use to wipe your behind.**
2. **How much to eat.**
3. **What is permissible to eat.**
4. **When to eat.**
5. **When not to eat.**
6. **When to pray.**
7. **How often to pray.**
8. **Sexual positions allowed.**
9. **Sexual positions forbidden.**
10. **Acts (sins) permitted by some and not others.**
11. **Sins committed can be simply forgiven.**
12. **Sins by one generation are not a sin by others.**
13. **Contraception not permitted.**
14. **Abortion not permitted.**
15. **Control over your own end of life not permitted.**
16. **You must believe in the only true God of that particular religion.**
17. **You must believe in the Angels of God.**
18. **You must believe in miracles.**
19. **You must believe in the holy book of that religion.**
20. **You must believe in the prophets of that religion.**

21. You must believe in the Day of Judgement.
22. You must believe in the Resurrection.
23. At certain times, you must fast.
24. You must believe life on earth is only a test for the afterlife.
25. God will reward the believers but punish the non-believers.
26. Some religions forbid gambling, alcohol, etc.
27. No adultery.
28. How you must dress.
29. How women must look or not look at men.
30. Women should not draw attention to themselves.
31. Women should not be too pleasant of speech toward other people.
32. Belief in reincarnation.
33. God will answer your prayers.
34. Faith above reason.
35. A Supreme Being over free will.
36. God controls everything.
37. Mary was a virgin.
38. Mary was not a virgin.
39. Polygamy is allowed.
40. Polygamy is not permitted.
41. God lives on the planet Kolab.
42. Cannot eat animals that walk on their paws.
43. Cannot eat animals that crawl on their belly.
44. Cannot eat animals from water that do not have fins and scales.
45. Cannot eat certain birds such as ostriches.
46. Cannot cook or drink milk with meat.
47. Cannot harvest, plant or eat grains and fruits at specific times.
48. Wine that is touched by a heathen is forbidden.
49. Any contact that leads to intermarriage is forbidden.

50. Specific punishment, including flogging, is permitted if forbidden food exceeding the size of an olive is consumed.

51. Washing one's face and one's hands up to the elbows, and the wiping of one's head and also one's feet up to the ankles, before commencing prayer.

52. If a person is in a state of sexual defilement, it is necessary to wash before prayer.

53. If a person is sick or travelling or coming out from relieving himself or has touched a woman and cannot find water, then rubbing the hands and face with pure earth is sufficient.

54. Stay away from women during their menstrual periods.

55. A woman may not pray during her menstrual period.

56. Wearing false hair, being tattooed, or plucking out facial hair or eyebrows by women are sins to be punished with death.

57. A man (husband) may unilaterally divorce his wife. A woman (wife) cannot. She needs the permission of a qadi judge.

58. All games of chance or playing of cards that cause financial gain or loss is prohibited.

59. It is forbidden to covert to another religion or leave this religion. It is known as apostasy and punishable by death.

60. The right hand must be used for eating or drinking.

61. Punishments include amputation of one/both hands for theft and stoning for adultery.

62. Homosexual sex is illegal and forbidden.

63. Jesus is the son of God.

64. God is a Trinity.

65. Jesus is the Messiah that the Jews were waiting for.

66. Jesus is not the Messiah, but only a man.

67. Jesus can walk on water, raise the dead, heal the sick and turn water into wine, etc.
68. Jesus will return someday.
69. The end of the world is near.
70. Blood transfusions are prohibited.
71. Saluting the flag or being involved in political activity is prohibited.
72. Prohibited from celebrating any of the following: Birthdays, Valentine's Day, Mother's Day, Christmas, Easter, etc.
73. Christ did return to earth in 1914.
74. Each member must be audited through the use of an "electropsychometer."
75. Believes in birth, death and rebirth.
76. God cannot be understood or explained.
77. The universe exists because God wills it to exist.
78. Must not lust, want worldly possessions, greed of money, show anger or demonstrate pride.
79. Must have uncut hair, wear a steel bracelet, use a wooden comb, wear cotton underwear, carry a small sword (kirpan).
80. The path of Evil leads to damnation, misery and ultimately Hell. The path of Righteousness leads to peace and everlasting happiness in Heaven.
81. The world, planet Earth, is only approximately six thousand years old.
82. Seventy-two virgins (or some other number) for blowing yourself up.
83. Confessing your sins to pedophile priests.
84. That an ark was able to hold two of every species on earth.
85. Seventy-five million years ago, Xenu brought billions of people to Earth in spacecraft resembling Douglas DC-8 airliners, stacked them around volcanoes, and detonated hydrogen bombs in the volcanoes.

86. Blacks are "the true Jews" and whites are "white devils" to be vanquished from the earth.
87. "Thou shalt not procreate." This religion further asserts four principal pillars: suicide, abortion, cannibalism ("strictly limited to consumption of the already dead"), and sodomy ("any sexual act not intended for procreation").
88. It is important to bury the afterbirth so that Satan does not use it to make a duplicate of the recently born child.
89. Furthermore, some aborted fetuses survive their abortion to live in the sewers, where they are being gathered and organized to take over the world.
90. People were once perfectly symmetrical and ambidextrous, but then a meteorite struck Earth and tilted its axis, causing handedness and shifting the heart off-centre in the chest.
91. Each of us has seven clones living in different parts of the world.
92. Women existed for many generations before they invented men through genetic manipulation.
93. Homo sapiens is the result of cloning experiments that were done on Mars using Homo erectus.
94. The Illuminati have nurtured a child, Satan's son, who was born on June 6, 1966, at the Dakota House on 72nd Street in New York to Jacqueline Kennedy Onassis of the Rothschild/Kennedy families. The Pope was present at the birth and performed necromantic ceremonies. The child was raised by former U.S. president Richard Nixon and now lives in Belgium, where it is hooked up bodily to a computer called "The Beast 3M" or "3666."
95. A talking snake, a burning bush and a parting of the sea.
96. A man was made from dirt, and a woman from the rib of a man.

97. **We should put special crackers and wine in our mouths; they will be magically transformed into the flesh and blood of Jesus, which we should then swallow despite taboos regarding cannibalism.**

98. **Baptism of the deceased.**

99. **At a certain holiday, you shake a chicken while praying and you can transfer your sins to the chicken.**

100. **Polluting devices such as televisions, computers, modern appliances, etc. are prohibited. Apparently phones are OK.**

The following excerpts are from Islam's holy books.

Qur'an [4:89] – And they wish that you should disbelieve like they have, then you will be equal; so take them not as your friends until they migrate in the Path of Allah. And if they turn away, then seize them and kill them wherever you find them, and take not from among them a friend or helper.

Hadith: contains religious interpretations often translated as prophetic 'traditions', of the reports, teachings, deeds and sayings of the Islamic prophet Muhammad.

Bukhari [52:260] – "The Prophet said, 'If somebody (a Muslim) discards his religion, kill him.' "

Bukhari [83:37] – "Allah's Apostle never killed anyone except in one of the following three situations: (1) A person who killed somebody unjustly, was killed (in Qisas,) (2) a married person who committed illegal sexual intercourse and (3) a man who fought against Allah and His Apostle and deserted Islam and became an apostate."

Bukhari [84:57] – "[In the words of] Allah's Apostle, 'Whoever changed his Islamic religion, then kill him.'"

Bukhari [89:271] – A man who embraces Islam, then reverts to Judaism is to be killed according to "the verdict of Allah and his apostle."

Bukhari [84:58] – "There was a fettered man beside Abu Muisa. Mu'adh asked, 'Who is this (man)?' Abu Muisa said, 'He was a Jew and became a Muslim and then reverted back to Judaism.' Then Abu Muisa requested Mu'adh to sit down but Mu'adh said, 'I will not sit down till he has been killed. This is the judgment of Allah and His Apostle (for such cases) and repeated it thrice.' Then Abu Musa ordered that the man be killed, and he was killed. Abu Musa added, 'Then we discussed the night prayers.'"

Bukhari [84:64-65] – "Allah's Apostle: 'During the last days there will appear some young foolish people who will say the best words but their faith will not go beyond their throats (i.e. they will have no faith) and will go out from (leave) their religion as an arrow goes out of the game. So, wherever you find them, kill them, for whoever kills them shall have reward on the Day of Resurrection.'"

Note: A growing number of Muslims have begun to reject the authority of the Hadith in favour of the primary authority of the Quran. They quote numerous verses of the Quran (e.g., 6:114, 6:115, 31:6, 45:6 and 77:50) to support their argument.

Qur'an:

[6:114] Shall I seek other than **GOD** as a source of law, when He has revealed to you this book fully detailed? Those who received the scripture recognize that it has been revealed from your Lord, truthfully. You shall not harbour any doubt.

[6:115] The word of your Lord is complete, in truth and justice. Nothing shall abrogate His words. He is the Hearer, the Omniscient.

[31:6] And of the people is he who buys the amusement of speech to mislead [others] from the way of Allah without knowledge and who takes it in ridicule. Those will have a humiliating punishment.

[45:6] These are the verses of Allah which We recite to you in truth. Then in what statement after Allah and His verses will they believe?

[77:50] Then in what statement after the Qur'an will they believe?

I'll leave it up to the reader to determine what to believe and what not to believe. Obviously, the Muslims themselves read these passages differently. Just like the Bible is read differently.

~

Words, Jargon and (Sesquipedalian) Mind Benders

"Words are singularly the most powerful force available to humanity. We can choose to use this force constructively with words of encouragement, or destructively using words of despair. Words have energy and power with the ability to help, to heal, to hinder, to hurt, to harm, to humiliate and to humble."

—Yehuda Berg, Rabbi

Words, Jargon and (Sesquipedalian) Mind Benders

"If you don't understand the language of the messenger, how could one ever understand the message?"

—Brian Hinkley

I don't know if it is particularly prevalent in atheism and religion, but since I developed an interest in these matters, I have found that the talkativeness of some experts on these subjects left me dizzy and in a state of puzzlement. At times the terminology used, while sounding like English, was totally incomprehensible to me. In listening to some podcasts or debates between authorities in the field of theology and science, I found I needed a dictionary in one hand and a thesaurus in the other in order to decipher what these folks were saying.

In other words, there appears to be a fondness by the highly educated to engage in long-winded exercises of unending eloquence by using a complicated form of communication. Some engage in what I call a "public display of linguistic masturbation." Then again, it was refreshing to listen to scholarly speakers who confronted this wordiness and translated their language for the benefit of the layperson into words that are more comprehensible.

At any rate, there are terms that you may encounter that you have never heard before; that is, if you have lived an ordinary life. If you have read this far in my book, congratulations! If you decide to pursue further reading material on this subject, you are hereby put on notice. There are some dandy terms that you may encounter. The fear of long words is otherwise known as "hippopotomonstrosesquipedaliophobia."

Don't be intimated. This list, along with their meanings, may help ease your anxiety.

Irreducible complexity (IC) is an argument by proponents of intelligent design that certain biological systems are too complex to have evolved from simpler, or "less complete" predecessors, through natural selection acting upon a series of advantageous naturally occurring, chance mutations. The argument is central to intelligent design, and is rejected by the scientific community at large, which overwhelmingly regards intelligent design as pseudoscience. Irreducible complexity is one of two main arguments used by intelligent design proponents, the other being specified complexity.

Confirmation bias is the tendency to search for, interpret, or prioritize information in a way that confirms one's beliefs or hypotheses. People display this bias when they gather or remember information selectively, or when they interpret it in a biased way. The effect is stronger for emotionally charged issues and for deeply entrenched beliefs. People also tend to interpret ambiguous evidence as supporting their existing position.

Religious believers are among those who are afflicted with this condition. Example: Many believe that if you pray long enough and hard enough, God will answer your prayers. If your prayers are never answered, this does not mean there is no God, it simply means that it was not God's will. In other words, whatever happens or doesn't happen, your bias will never be altered, regardless of proof or evidence to the contrary.

Transubstantiation is the change whereby, according to the teaching of the Catholic Church, the bread and the wine used in the sacrament of the Eucharist become, not merely as by a sign or a figure but also in actual reality, the body and blood of Christ. The Catholic Church teaches that the substance or reality of the bread is changed into that of the body of Christ and the substance of the wine into that of his blood.

If Catholics believe this is true, why don't they also consider themselves to be practicing cannibalism — the eating of the flesh of another person — every time they eat the flesh and drink the blood of Christ? And, even if they have some way to get around the label of cannibalism, from a purely subjective point of view, this practice (ritual) is really quite disgusting to me. If I was a Catholic and believed in transubstantiation, every time I took the Eucharist I would be grossed out.

Some Catholics cling to the belief that the Eucharist represents only a symbol of eating flesh and drinking blood. Well, that still makes them cannibals, if only symbolic cannibals. Participation in this ritual as a metaphorical representation of eating Christ's body then makes Catholics metaphorical cannibals. They simply have no easy way out of this predicament, either as symbolic cannibals or real cannibals. Either way, the morality of eating another person seems to me to be against humanity...and common sense.

In some societies, especially tribal societies, cannibalism is a cultural norm. Consumption of a person from within the same community is called endocannibalism; ritual cannibalism of the recently deceased can be part of the grieving process, or a way of guiding the souls of the dead into the bodies of living descendants.

Exocannibalism is the consumption of a person from outside the community, usually as a celebration of victory against a rival tribe. Both types of cannibalism can also be fuelled by the belief that eating a person's flesh or internal organs will endow the cannibal with some of the characteristics of the deceased. Perhaps Catholics believe if you eat the body of Christ you will become Christ-like.

Disambiguation refers to the removal of ambiguity by making something clear. Disambiguation narrows down the meaning of words. This word makes sense if you break it down. "Dis" means "not," "ambiguous" means "unclear," and the ending "-tion" makes it a noun.

Transcendental means beyond common thought or experience; mystical or supernatural.

Proselytize means to convert or attempt to convert (someone) from one religion, belief or opinion to another.

Cognitive dissonance, in psychology, is the mental stress or discomfort experienced by an individual who holds two or more contradictory beliefs, ideas or values at the same time, or is confronted by new information that conflicts with existing beliefs, ideas or values.

Ockham's razor is a principle that states the simplest explanation is the most plausible one. (If you want to give your brain a real workout, go ahead and study this concept further. Be warned, however; it may make you go crazy.)

A **presupposition** is an implicit assumption about the world or background belief relating to an utterance whose truth is taken for granted in discourse.

Consequentialism refers to those moral theories that hold that the consequences of one's conduct are the true basis for any judgment about the morality of that conduct. Thus, from a consequentialist standpoint, a morally right act (or omission) is one that will produce a good outcome, or consequence. This view is often expressed as the aphorism *"The ends justify the means."*

Deontology accepts the rightness or wrongness of one's conduct from the character of the behaviour itself rather than the outcomes of the conduct.

Virtue ethics focuses on the character of the agent rather than on the nature or consequences of the act (or omission) itself.

The differences among these three approaches to morality tend to lie more in the way moral dilemmas are approached than in the moral conclusions reached. For example, a consequentialist may argue that lying is wrong because of the negative consequences produced by lying — though a consequentialist may allow that certain foreseeable consequences might make lying acceptable. A deontologist might argue that lying is *always* wrong, regardless of any potential "good" that might come from lying. A virtue ethicist, however, would focus less on lying in any particular instance and instead consider what a decision to tell a lie or not says about one's character and moral behaviour.

All of the above was accessed from the following website: http://www.princeton.edu/~achaney/tmve/wiki100k/docs/C onsequentialism.html

Utilitarianism: An ethical philosophy in which the happiness of the greatest number of people in the society is considered the greatest good. According to this philosophy, an action is morally right if its consequences lead to happiness (absence of pain), and wrong if it ends in unhappiness (pain).

From:
http://www.businessdictionary.com/definition/utilitarianism.html#ixzz3Lu9iNh1c

Omnidimensional may not be an actual word. God is described as omni many things, such as omnipotent, omnipresent, omniscient, omnicompetent, omnibenevolent. Perhaps "omnidemensional" is as good as any to describe God. I would add "omnikiller. "

Anthropomorphize means to assign human characteristics to nonhuman things, such as deities.

I don't have a lot of time for New Age mystics…and this is the only space I will give it in my book. I'm sure everyone understands exactly what this following quote means in plain English…I don't.

"There is no fixed physical reality, no single perception of the world, just numerous ways of interpreting world views as dictated by one's nervous system and the specific environment of our planetary existence."
—Deepak Chopra

OK, I'm not even going there. As far as I am concerned, religion itself is enough hocus pocus. This New Age nonsense, the world of psychics who talk to the dead, fortune tellers, and a whole other crew of mystics, are plain and simple con artists who prey on naïveté.

These charlatans who fleece innocent victims with their outrageous claims are no different than religious evangelists, except religion gets to do it with our taxes.

A senior (opportunistic) politician friend of mine once said to me, as we were sitting at a community meeting, waiting for his time to address the audience, *"Watch me get this crowd up on their feet applauding and cheering."*

Standing at the lectern, he started speaking, and it went something like this:

"Ladies and gentlemen, members of the board, platform guests and boys and girls, let me say how proud I am to be here today. But more importantly how proud I am of the work you are doing to improve this community. We live in a world today where people don't care enough about others. But you folks have set a shining example of what it means to care about your community. There are those in government today who care more about being re-elected than serving the community in which they represent. Some of my colleagues in government can take a lesson from you folks here. Take Mary Gibbons, for example; her contribution has touched the lives of many and improved them more than words can express. Your own John Anderson is a constant reminder of self-sacrifice and goodness. The time he has committed to each and every one of you, often in ways that you will never know, goes unheralded. This is what it means to be a community. This is what it means to help one another. You have all done yourself proud, and I applaud you on your efforts... No, you should applaud yourselves. I want you to stand up right now and shake the hand of your neighbour sitting beside you. Then give yourselves one great big round of applause."

He then sat down beside me as the auditorium erupted in a cacophony of noise, laughter and raucous cheers. I asked him, *"What did you really say?"* He replied. *"Absolutely nothing. I should have been a preacher."*

The Lesson: Words can be used to confuse, bait, manipulate or clarify. You can choose to believe in reality or be duped into a world of make-believe. All you need is the courage and knowledge to know one from the other.

~

Discrimination against Atheists

"Injustice anywhere is a threat to justice everywhere."

—Martin Luther King Jr.

Discrimination against Atheists

"Atheists, humanists and liberals" now targeted as a distinct minority by "hate campaigns" Report

International Humanist and Ethical Union (IHEU)
December 10, 2014

Non-religious people are being targeted by "hate campaigns" in countries around the world, as a distinct minority group, the latest edition of the *Freedom of Thought Report* has found.

The report claims that the "hate speech" against atheists does not come exclusively from reactionary or radical religious leaders, but increasingly from political leaders, including heads of state.

Published today (10 December, 2014) by the International Humanist and Ethical Union (IHEU), the *Freedom of Thought Report* states: "In 2014, in addition to laws such as those targeting 'apostasy' and 'blasphemy', we have seen a marked increase in specific targeting of 'atheists' and 'humanism' as such, using these terms in a broadly correct way (the users know what they are saying) but with intent clearly borne of ignorance or intolerance toward these groups."

Cases covered in the report include the Malaysian Prime Minister Najib Razak, who this year labelled "humanism and secularism as well as liberalism" as "deviant" and a threat to Islam and the state itself, in a speech where he also denied that Malaysians had any right to "apostasy" (leaving Islam).

Saudi Arabia comes into criticism for a new law equating "atheism" with "terrorism". The very first article of the kingdom's new terror regulations banned: "Calling for atheist thought in any form, or calling into question the fundamentals of the Islamic religion".

The *Freedom of Thought Report* annually surveys and rates every country in the world for anti-atheist persecution. Almost all countries discriminate against the non-religious, in some cases through religious privilege or legal exemptions, with the worst countries taking children from atheist parents, or with laws mandating death sentences for "apostates" (in 13 Islamic states).

The 2014 edition of the report notes: "This year will be marked by a surge in this phenomenon of state officials and political leaders agitating specifically against non-religious people, just because they have no religious beliefs, in terms that would normally be associated with hate speech or social persecution against ethnic or religious minorities."

For the complete report go to:

http://freethoughtreport.com/download-the-report/

Unenforceable ban on atheists holding public office still on the books in 8 states

By Stephanie McNeal

Published July 16, 2014 – FoxNews.com

The U.S. Constitution says religious tests cannot be required to hold public office. But if you read through the constitutions of eight states, they seem to require just that. It's strange but true. Provisions barring atheists from holding public office are written into the constitutions of those states, even though they can't be enforced.

That's because the Supreme Court ruled in 1961 that a Maryland man who was appointed as a notary public did not have to declare his belief in God to be eligible for the office, which was required under the state's constitution. The justices ruled unanimously that forcing the man to do so would violate his rights under the First and Fourteenth Amendments.

The case, Torcaso v. Watkins, made enforcement of the provisions illegal, but merely allowing them to remain on the books does not violate the U.S. Constitution. So they remain in Arkansas, Maryland, Mississippi, North Carolina, Pennsylvania, South Carolina, Tennessee and Texas.

Mississippi's Constitution states, *"No person who denies the existence of a Supreme Being shall hold any office in this state."* Arkansas' Constitution goes even further; it bars atheists from testifying in court.

Tennessee's bars atheists from office, but, curiously, the state also forbids ministers. Its provision states that any minister of the gospel or priest of any denomination is barred from public office because they "ought not to be diverted from the great duties of their functions."

Dave Muscato, a spokesman for American Atheists, said it is *"fair and right" that the Supreme Court declared the provisions illegal, calling them "blatantly discriminatory, immoral, and un-American."*

He said having the provisions on the books is a *"stark reminder"* of the discrimination atheists have faced in America.

"While the social stigma still exists and black-and-white laws on the books do lend informal credibility to the stigma, insofar as it's our place to as (nonprofit) to speak on the issue, we encourage our lawmakers to spend as much time as possible making sure that religion and government stay separate in their work now, and that atheists are not discriminated against in the present," he told FoxNews.com in an email.

The provisions still cause controversy. North Carolina's caused a stir in 2009 when Cecil Bothwell, an atheist, was elected to the city council in the city of Asheville.

Bothwell's critics said he should be barred from office because of the state Constitution's guidelines, but ultimately he was sworn in. One of those critics, Southern heritage activist H.K. Edgerton, told FoxNews.com the provision barring atheists should be enforced because it *"is in the North Carolina State Constitution, and is law."*

"The Asheville, North Carolina City Council has placed itself above the law for two terms with Cecil Bothwell sitting there passing rules and regulations and dictating law unlawfully," he said.

Muscato said it is unlikely lawmakers will ever seek to get the provisions taken out of the state constitutions, as there is rarely a push to remove unenforceable laws from the books.

"However, having them on the books, even though they aren't enforceable, is a stark reminder that our country once considered an atheist so unfit for office that it was proper to bar a person from serving the people just because the candidate wasn't indoctrinated into believing," he said.

Atheist lawmakers are rare in the U.S. A Pew Research poll found only one current member of Congress, Rep. Kyrsten Sinema, D-Ariz., said she was *"unaffiliated"* with a religion. Ten other lawmakers refused to answer the question or said they did not know.

Former Rep. Pete Stark, D-Calif., was the only open atheist in Congress from 1973 to 2013. He was defeated in the Democratic primary by current Rep. Eric Swalwell when he ran for re-election after redistricting in 2012.

---

11 Things Atheists Couldn't Do Because They Didn't Believe In God

The Huffington Post By Nick Wing Posted: 01/16/2014 8:08 am EST Updated: 01/25/2014

I have drastically condensed this article. For the complete article go to:

http://www.huffingtonpost.com/2014/01/16/atheists-discrimination_n_4413593.html

Here are 11 things atheists couldn't — and in many cases still can't — do because they didn't believe in God.

1. Live. Atheists in 13 countries face execution under the law if they openly express their beliefs or reject the official state religion — Islam in all of these cases.

2. Run for office. Not believing in God is political poison, at least if you express that belief openly. While the most severe mistreatment of atheists may take place in fundamentalist nations, political discrimination is pervasive across the U.S. Despite polling that has shown non believers making up an increasingly large part of the country, there isn't a single admitted atheist in Congress right now, and by most counts, there's only one in all of the state legislatures across the nation.

Furthermore, despite constitutional restrictions on "religious tests" for holding public office, six states have laws on the books barring non believers. These laws aren't technically in effect, but they don't need to be. Not believing in God is such a volatile political issue that a simple meeting with people who have ties to atheist groups can expose a candidate to a brutal smear campaign.

3. Be trusted by their peers. Discrimination against atheists doesn't appear only in the political realm, though it is quite clear there. A poll taken during the 2012 election season found that only 54 percent of Americans would vote for a "well-qualified" atheist presidential candidate. While this was the highest total since Gallup began asking the question in 1958, atheism proved the biggest negative influence on a hypothetical candidate's viability, with fewer respondents saying they would be willing to vote for an atheist than either a gay or a Muslim candidate.

4. Be respected by their leaders or neighbors. During his swearing-in speech in 2011, Alabama Gov. Robert Bentley (R) threw inclusiveness out the window when he made these comments about religion:

"So anybody here today who has not accepted Jesus Christ as their savior, I'm telling you, you're not my brother and you're not my sister, and I want to be your brother," he said.

It's hard to imagine any other class of people, especially one so large — we're not just talking non believers here, but people of all non-Christian faiths — being so casually and expressly dismissed.

5. Have a job. Not believing in God could make it harder to get a job, though that would of course require a would-be employer to be aware of a candidate's non theistic beliefs.

6. Get custody of their children. If atheists can't be trusted to be good employees, they *certainly* can't be trusted to be responsible parents.

Over the past few decades, there have been many documented cases of judges either denying parents custody rights because of their apparent disinterest in organized religion, or in other cases, of atheist parents being ordered to attend church so that their children can undergo "systematic spiritual training."

7. Volunteer in their communities. When the Upstate Atheists, a charity organization in Spartanburg, S.C., offered to lend a hand volunteering at a local soup kitchen last year, they were surprised to hear that the director of the facility would have rather resigned than work alongside godless members of the community.

8. Advertise their beliefs, or lack thereof. The battle over the place of God in advertising has frequently led to broader questions about discrimination against atheists.

In 2011, a judge ruled that the Central Arkansas Transit Authority had violated the free speech rights of a local atheist group when it denied the group's request to launch an ad campaign on city buses. The ad organization that worked with the transit authority had regularly approved religious ads.

9. Participate in life without violating their beliefs. While the Establishment Clause of the U.S. Constitution is supposed to ensure a clear separation of church and state, the two frequently intermix, much to the disapproval of non believers.

This manifests itself in a variety of ways, from the inclusion of the word "God" in various mandatory pledges and on the face of U.S. currency, to compulsory religious-based sessions that atheists have been unconstitutionally forced to take part in.

10. Create an organization. Groups of atheists have regularly been denied the opportunity to form recognized clubs at public schools around the nation. While this difficulty is not universal, it is common. Administrators have been known to erect procedural hurdles to discourage non believers from organizing, or in some cases, simply rejected their applications.

11. Become a Boy Scout. This one's pretty straightforward. The Boy Scouts of America still prohibits atheists from joining its ranks. Scouts must pledge to "do my duty to God and my country," and the BSA has resisted calls to remove religion from the oath.

Scouts have even been asked to leave their troops after their non theistic beliefs were discovered. In 2009, Eagle Scout Neil Polzin was fired from his job as an aquatics director at a Boy Scouts camp after his role with a secular student group was uncovered.

Outrageous Incidents of Discrimination against Non-believers

AlterNet / *By Greta Christina December 20, 2012*

Again, I have condensed this article. For the complete article go to:

http://www.alternet.org/belief/6-outrageous-incidents-discrimination-against-nonbelievers

1: Alber Saber, Egypt. Alber Saber, the 27-year-old atheist activist, blogger, and reported administrator of the Egyptian Atheists Facebook page, was arrested after a mob swarmed outside his home demanding his arrest for insulting religion. Saber was then attacked in prison, after a guard told the other prisoners what he had been charged with.

2: Alexander Aan, Indonesia. In January 2012, Indonesian civil servant Alexander Aan was attacked by an entirely different mob, after he criticized Islam on Facebook and said he'd left the religion and become an atheist. Following the attack, Aan was arrested for insulting religion (i.e., blasphemy), electronic transmission of defamatory statements (i.e., blasphemy via the Internet), and false reporting on an official form.

3: Phillipos Loizos, Greece. In September 2012, Phillipos Loizos was arrested in Evia, Greece, on charges of posting "malicious blasphemy and religious insult" on Facebook.

His crime? Creating a Facebook page making fun of Elder Paisios, the late Greek Orthodox monk revered by many as a prophet — a page referring to Paisios as Pastistios, connecting him with the satirical atheist faux-religion Pastafarianism, and replacing his face with an image of the Greek beef dish pastitsio. Seriously.

5: Fazil Say, Turkey. Of course, sometimes it is a problem of Muslim extremists. If you know the world of classical and jazz piano, you might already know of Fazil Say: he is apparently widely renowned in that world. He is also an atheist. On June 1, 2012, he was arrested and charged with insulting Islamic values, via the fearsome and formidable medium of Twitter.

6: Jabeur Mejri and Ghazi Beji, Tunisia. Seven and a half years: that's the prison sentence given to atheists Jabeur Mejri and Ghazi Beji in Tunisia in March 2012, for posting cartoons of Muhammad on Facebook.

Beji got lucky, and got the hell out of the country: he is still being sought as a fugitive by Tunisian authorities.

There are many other stories demonstrating acts of discrimination against atheists. Most of the time it is ordinary or unknown people who is subjected to someone's prejudices. Occasionally a well known atheist personality may encounter acts of discrimination.

The following story involving Richard Dawkins appeared on the American Humanists Association website: http://americanhumanist.org/Press/Naughty_Awareness_A ds/Stories

Richard Dawkins Dissed By Country Club — Rochester Hills, MI (2011)

"The managers of the Wyndgate Country Club decided to cancel a fundraising event featuring Richard Dawkins, the well-known evolutionary biologist, author and atheist. The cancellation came after one of the club's officials saw Dawkins on "The O'Reilly Factor," discovering for the first time he was an atheist. The official decided that was cause enough to cancel the confirmed engagement, which had to be quickly moved elsewhere."

"The AHA is assisting the Center for Inquiry in a possible legal response."

I am left to ask in bewilderment — what are people afraid of? Fear of atheism is like all other fears — a fear of the unknown. People fear that which they don't understand. Understanding usually helps to allay people's fears, though I suspect many people simply do not want to understand what it means to be an atheist and a humanist.

Prehistoric man had many fears. He feared animals, fire, lighting and thunder, among many other things. These fears were borne out of ignorance or a basic necessity to protect oneself. I suppose folks who fear atheists think we are a threat to their religion.

In one sense, perhaps they are right. Yet, atheists really don't care what a person believes or doesn't believe. However, the freedom to express one's opinions and pursue life should be available to all, regardless of their beliefs or non beliefs.

It is here religion and atheism part company. Many religions have a desire or, they believe, a mandate to impose their beliefs upon others. While atheists will express their opinions, defend their positions or even disagree strongly with religious dogma, they do not proselytize or discriminate. Some religions feel they must regularly convert you or, as we have seen, discriminate against you. Still others will actually have you killed if you do not subscribe to their beliefs.

Religious extremist and fundamentalists present a real obstacle to society's progressive advancement and logical thinking. They are wired to the past. These people see issues as black or white, right and wrong, dos and don'ts...heaven or hell. There is no room for questions or reasoned discussion. The word of God is absolute and is therefore sacrosanct. To question the word of God is tantamount to blasphemy in the eyes of the religious fanatics.

Religion describes their message as inspirational. Inspirational is defined as that which makes one want to do something, or that which gives someone an idea about what to do or create. Religion describes inspirational as a divine force or influence. It is time for atheists to claim the word "inspirational" as their message. The message of atheism inspires people to be their own person. It encourages one to think, challenge and question; not to be submissive, blind and obedient to a controlling dogma.

I agree with Richard Dawkins; much of what some of the religious believe is a delusion...a delusion that often finds its origins in fear and an unrealistic belief in an afterlife.

~

Best Resource Material
(For the layman)

Best Books

1. *The God Delusion*, by Richard Dawkins
2. *God Is Not Great*, by Christopher Hitchens
3. *The End of Faith*, by Sam Harris
4. *The Born Again Skeptic's Guide to the Bible*, by Ruth Hurmence Green (Available only through Freedom from Religion Foundation.)
5. *How to Get into the Bible*, by Stephen M. Miller (I grant you, this book has a religious bent, but I found it candid and easy to read for the layman, with plenty of pictures, and it is great for a quick reference. I'm sure the author did not intend it to be a resource for atheists or to be funny, but I found parts of it hilarious.)
6. *Atheism For Dummies*, by Dale McGowan
7. *Drunk with Blood: God's Killings in the Bible*, by Steve Wells

---

I would also recommend reading the Holy Bible and the works of Richard Carrier, Victor J. Stenger and D.M. Murdock (aka Acharya S.) However, a layman may find these to be tough sledding and difficult to read. Yet, if you listen to Richard Carrier speak on the issue he can translate difficult-to-understand concepts into ordinary language. I did not find that was the case with his writing.

The Great Agnostic, better known as Robert G. Ingersoll, is without a doubt a man ahead of his times. If you access his written material or listen to some of his speeches (dubbed by others), you cannot help but be impressed.

His language is poetry. His oratory must have been spellbinding. If he were alive today, I would travel anywhere in the world just to hear one of his speeches.

There is only one caveat for the layman. He speaks in a language of another age. Ordinary people may in fact be turned off by his eloquence, which is better suited for the late nineteenth century.

If you do nothing else after reading this far, I urge you to check out this website:
https://www.secularhumanism.org/index.php/1168
and watch the two videos featured.

Best Movies

1. *The Life of Brian*, by Monty Python
2. *Religulous*, starring Bill Maher
3. *September Dawn*, starring Jon Voight
4. *The Invention of Lying*, starring Ricky Gervais
5. *Higher Ground*, starring Vera Farmiga

Best Websites

1. https://www.secularhumanism.org/index.php/1168
2. http://www.jesusneverexisted.com/index.html
   (and this link):
   http://www.jesusneverexisted.com/brutal.htm
3. http://truthbeknown.com/
4. https://richarddawkins.net/
5. http://godisimaginary.com/
6. http://www.thebestschools.org/blog/2011/12/01/50-top-atheists-in-the-world-today/
7. http://infidels.org/
8. http://www.evilbible.com/
9. http://www.greenwych.ca/bible-a.htm

10. http://www.skepticsannotatedbible.com/
11. http://www.centerforinquiry.net/
12. http://southernskeptic.com/

Best Podcasts

The first five podcasts listed are good resources for most audiences.

1. http://ffrf.org/news/radio (Nice)
2. http://www.thethinkingatheist.com/podcast (Intelligent)
3. http://www.atheist-experience.com/archive /?full=1#table (Mental workout)
4. http://atheism101podcast.com/ (Easygoing)
5. http://dogmadebate.com/ (Pushes the envelope)

The language starts to get a bit salty, because these folks are the salt of the earth.

6. http://noreligionrequired.com/category/podcast/ (I love Ms. Ashley & Bobby C. too!)
7. http://barroomatheist.podbean.com/ (No punches pulled)

Hide the children. Nothing is off-limits.

8. http://aoa.fm/ (Get ready to duck when Cash gets riled)
9. http://dissonancepod.com/ (Morbid, hilarious and unrestrained)
10. http://scathingatheist.com/podcast/ (Machine-gun style diatribe — try to keep up)

~

Conclusion and Epilogue

This depiction of the Roman god Janus is appropriate to represent **all religions** today. Religion is bound by its rotting past, which it cannot escape and, by all accounts, is an indictment of its horrifying history. Many Christian religions attempt to ignore much of the disgusting parts of the Bible's Old Testament; hence, the face of the old man looking backward with his eyes closed.

Christianity, in an attempt to reinvent itself, has a fresh, new face that relies more upon the New Testament and a look to the future. Considering the historical record of inhumane treatment of women, which many religions continue today, it is deceptive to have the face of a woman looking forward to the future with her eyes open. Notwithstanding this attempt at renewal, the picture shows how religion is crumbling from both ends. The hourglass on the top of the picture indicates that time is running out for ancient beliefs based upon myths and superstition.

Conclusion and Epilogue

"Religion is the music — science is the lyrics"
—Brian Hinkley

As religion continues its appeal to human emotions, offers a glorious nirvana in the afterlife, and sells more sizzle than steak, religion will remain part of the human condition for many years to come.

When people believe with all their hearts and all their souls, and beyond all reason, that $2 + 2 = 5$, there can be no dialogue. Such is the case with devout believers of religion. Religious apologists cannot be convinced that $2 + 2 = 4$ if they believe the Bible, or their special holy book, tells them the answer is 5. As a non-believer, it is not my mission to convert anyone to any particular philosophy, belief or dogma. Some religions have as their mission to convert anyone and everyone to their belief system. In short, they proselytize. They want to tell you what to believe and how you should live.

Religion is mainly an emotional appeal. Science mainly relies on logic and reason. Humans are a mix of both. Whichever can strike the proper balance of emotion and reason will succeed in winning the minds and the hearts of the people on this planet.

As an atheist, I will simply put forth my position, using reason and logic, that $2 + 2 = 4$. If a Catholic Christian wants to believe the correct answer is 5, and an evangelical Christian wants to believe the correct answer is 6, and a Muslim wants to believe the correct answer is 7, then it becomes futile to argue or debate the issue.

A. C. Grayling, in his book *The God Argument*, writes the following on pages 160–161 in the chapter "Humanism and the Good Life."

"There is no suggestion in any of the foregoing that the way to make a good life is to adopt and adhere to someone else's idea of a good life: on the contrary. This is the point of insisting that people must think for themselves. **Bertrand Russell's** *witticism that* **'most people would rather die than think and most people do'** *is intended to focus attention on a too common human propensity, namely, the desire for other people to do the hard yards of working out what is right and wrong, and of finding out what to think and do as a result.*

"That is one of the reasons why religion has survived into the modern world: it tells people what to think and do, gratifying their reluctance to make the effort, or to take the risk, of achieving self-understanding and on that basis choosing a course that would be a fulfilling expression of their individual talents for living well. In wanting a quick answer to 'what should I do, how shall I live?' people grab a one-size-fits-all model from a shelf in the ideas supermarket, and leave it at that....

"[G]iven that each individual has his or her own set of talents and capacities, there might be as many different possible good lives as there are people to live them. It is a false view purveyed by monolithic ideologies — the ideologies that say there is one great truth and one right way to live, and everyone must conform, be the same, do the same, obey, submit — that there is only one kind of good life and that it is the same for all."

Grayling goes further in describing how to live the "good life" and uses terms such as "meaningful," "purposeful," "positive," "fruitful," "flourishing," "intimacy," "love," "friendship," "doing," "making," "learning," "honesty," "authenticity," "autonomy," "responsibility," "quality," "satisfying" and "integrity," among other characteristics, that help to demonstrate the meaning and philosophy of a good life…all without the necessity of a religion or a god.

In my life, I have known many decent, upright and moral Christians and Jews and a few Muslims. All of these people are good people. They mean no harm but only wish goodness for all of humanity.

Most of this book dealt with Christianity. First, I want to now take a moment to relate some information about a Jewish rabbi, whom I highly respect and admire, notwithstanding his religion. Secondly, I will share with you my personal experience with a Muslim.

Rabbi Bernard Baskin, of Hamilton, Ontario, is a scholar, and a very wise man. I believe he is a humanist in the broadest sense of the word. Yet, I am sure he is often misunderstood. If you were to meet him for the first time there is a reserved demeanour about him. All of humanity, religious and non-religious, are the better for his intelligence and inspiration. His comforting words can never be mistaken. They are poetry that wraps around you with warmth and kindness.

Rabbi Baskin's writings could almost be entirely accepted by any atheist-humanist, even if the good Rabbi always manages to insert some reference to God in most of his writings. The following compassionate and thoughtful article appeared in the March 22, 2013 edition of the *Hamilton Spectator*.

BASKIN: Death, grief and life

"Over the years, it has been my sad duty to officiate at many funerals. I have met with families in their moments of deepest grief. I have witnessed many approaches to sorrow. From this broad experience, certain basic ideas and concepts emerge.

"In the first place, I have learned that it is good and necessary for a person to express grief. This sounds simple enough. But there is a tendency in our age is to be ashamed of showing our feelings.

"When we call upon a friend who has sustained a loss, we try to talk about everything except the reality of death. Death is uncomfortable. It disturbs us; we want as little anxiety as possible.

"We may not accept all the teachings of modern psychology, but this much is certainly true: when we repress our natural emotions we create abnormal reactions. Often these emerge later in life as physical pain or mental distress.

"Second, there is a widespread tendency to say what is improper to a person who is mourning. Out of mistaken good will, we say that time is a great healer, or that God works in mysterious ways, or that love will come again.

"These well-meant platitudes leave the mourner confused and disconcerted. The sorrow, after all, is genuine and real and the mourner needs to feel and express it.

"The Talmud advises that the comforters should not utter words of consolation until the mourner speaks.

"Third, it is necessary to respond to the challenge of life, to pick up the threads of daily existence once again. Unwisely, some mourners withdraw into a realm of exaggerated grief and excessive mourning. They wrap around themselves the gloomy garments of extended sorrow rather than face the truth that life must go on.

"Shakespeare wrote 'Moderate lamentation is the right of the dead; excessive grief the enemy of the living.'

"Rabbi Jacob Rudin left us these thoughtful words, 'To ask of death that it never come is futile, but it is not futility to pray that when death does come it may take us from a world one corner of which is a little better because we were there.'

"Life is a gift and to die emotionally or spiritually because of the loss of a loved one is to compound or double the loss.

"The British novelist Margaret Jameson reminds us how each of our days is precious and irretrievable. 'The past is gone beyond prayer and every minute we spend in the vain effort to anticipate the future is a moment lost. There is only one world: the one pressing against you at this minute. There is only one minute in which you are alive: this minute — here and now. The only way to live is by accepting each minute as an unrepeatable miracle. Which is exactly what it is — a miracle and unrepeatable.'

"Finally, in contemplating the life of a loved one, the values that really matter and persist are character, integrity, reputation and family relationships.

"A good character is the fruit of personal exertion. We don't inherit it from our parents.

"It doesn't come to us automatically because of where we live, or how much formal education we possess, or the nature of our work, or the size of our income.

"After our time on earth we carry nothing away with us except the memory of our character, our good deeds, our good name."

Bernard Baskin is Rabbi Emeritus of Temple Anshe Sholom in Hamilton and is an occasional contributor to The Spectator's Books and Comment pages.

Except for the few religious references, I find very little to take issue with this wise and thoughtful advice. I often think that other than a belief in a god, a good religious person and a good atheist-humanist have much in common.

The few Muslims that I have met seemed terribly serious and I didn't understand them at all until a few years ago. I listened to Tarek Fatah on 1010 am Radio, Toronto. This man is a most unusual and interesting human being. Tarek is a Muslim with a sense of connection, friendship, and understanding. Something else about Tarek, which I find is a rarity among Muslims – he has a sense of humour.

This discussion now leads me to Mohamed, not the Prophet, but rather an acquaintance. For approximately a year I would have the occasional street chat with Mohamed. He lived in my neighbourhood with his wife and son. His wife didn't speak much, but Mohamed was quite friendly. I believe he was a professor at McMaster University. Most of our chats were simply neighbourhood greetings, talk about the weather and other small talk. One day I helped him out with a minor household repair.

He then became quite friendly. One day he invited my wife and I to have dinner with his family at a local Muslim restaurant. It was an enjoyable evening and we shared pleasantries. I remained skeptical of Mohamed's motives. As we became more comfortable with each other I posed a rather indelicate question. I asked Mohamed; *"Are you trying to convert me to Islam?"* Mohamed laughed and said no he wasn't.

The next question required more courage on my part. I said, *"Mohamed, I don't understand Islam and perhaps you can answer a concern that I have."* It was almost as though he knew what I was about to ask. I hesitated and thought about asking him; *"Does the Muslim religion commit their followers to kill non-believers?"* It was as though Mohamed read my mind. He chuckled, and I'll paraphrase Mohamed, but basically he explained that there are all kinds of Muslims who understand Islam differently; just as you have many Christians who believe in their own form of Christianity. Most Muslims want the same thing most other people want – to work, raise a family and have a good life and Islam is our guidance to responsibility.

I was relieved that he wasn't trying to convert me, and a whole lot more relieved that he didn't want to kill me. A few months later he moved to Toronto and we lost contact with each other.

It was an interesting experience and demonstrates that it is important to talk with one another, regardless of race, religion or creed. It is only through dialogue and conversation that we learn to understand and accept the differences of others. Accepting that others have different beliefs, means we can still live with each other, while still maintaining our own beliefs or non-beliefs, as the case may be.

This may be a very poor analogy, as sportsmanship seems to be lacking in today's world of professional sports. Opposing beliefs, can in some respects, be compared to opposing sports teams. I used to play a little football, basketball and baseball. One of my coaches said to me, something like this; *"I want you to hit that son-of-a-bitch as hard as you can and knock that bastard to the ground."* He then said; *"After the play is over, you go to him, offer your hand, help him up, and pat him on the shoulder."* He added; *"If someone beats you at a play; I want you to congratulate him, and the next time be damn sure to beat him."* *"Do you understand,"* he barked.

When you are instructed in this fashion, you have only one response; *"Yes sir!"* That is sportsmanship - something that we all need to learn (including me) in this discussion of the differences with the religious and atheists.

It would be nice if we all played by the same rules, unfortunately this is not so. Wishing it otherwise will not make it happen. The 9-11 horror changed people. Many people have developed a jaundiced view of religion, and its place in the affairs of our life, governments and the influence it has over world affairs. I hold the opinion that religion, and the practice thereof, is your own personal decision. If you want to pray to one god or another that's your right and none of my business. If you want to believe in the supernatural; knock yourself out. If you want to give your money to the church, well it is your money; give it to whoever or whatever you want.

Then I began to see how religion involved itself in the affairs of government. First it was through stealth, later through the backdoor, now it seems, in many places, one cannot distinguish religion from government as they are intertwined.

The influence religion has over government policies results in religious dogma becoming law. This unhealthy influence has spread to our public schools and government institutions. All the while tax dollars are being siphoned off to support religious goals and purposes, which many do not support. In some countries religion is the government and the government is the religion. Some would change our secular governments into theocracies, if they could.

With all the nonsense that fills their holy books, it is too easy to scoff, laugh and ridicule all the fairy tales, fallacies and insanity contained within their pages. Then, after the laughter dies down; I stop myself, pause and realize these people are serious. As D.M. Murdock said on page 262 of her book "Who was Jesus":

*"To reiterate, this issue is not to be taken lightly, as the threat of the global destruction of civilization by religious fanatics looms larger by the day. The devisers of clever fables have, in fact, established a bizarre and dangerous fairytale that is setting up the entire world for a decimating holocaust, apocalypse and Armageddon the like of which we have never seen before. With its constant portrayal of "End Times" scenes of death and destruction, the fundamentalist Christian perception of reality, which incorporates the Muslim and Jewish paradigms as well, constitutes a deleterious delusion that teaches a variety of doctrines incompatible with the love for life but repeatedly calling for a cosmic battle that ends all life. With its *eschatological doctrines of the Second Coming, Rapture and End Times, the Christian myth is, in the final analysis, unsustainable."*

---

eschatological: This is another $10.00 word that is new to me. It means a branch of theology concerned with the final events in the history of the world or of humankind.

Is Ms. Murdock correct? This is what Jesus said:

Matthew 10: 34-36 *"Do not think that I have come to bring peace to the earth. I have not come to bring peace, but a sword. For I have come to set a man against his father, and a daughter against her mother, and a daughter-in-law against her mother-in-law. And a person's enemies will be those of his own household."*

Religious apologists tie themselves in knots trying to explain away the obvious intent of this statement. These are the words that could only come out of the mouth of a monster.

I come to the conclusion that we are involved in a race. The problem is that most of the people of the world do not realize that the race is underway. We are in a race to save the world, and the future of mankind and our planet, from destruction. Not from a world-wide pandemic or an asteroid from space or even climate change, but rather from religious zealots.

We live in a world were billions of people have no idea of the maniacal writings contained within the holy books of the various religions. Most people, who attend church, have never read the Bible. They only hear about the nice parts of the Bible. Preachers deliberately avoid or sugar-coat the horror stories.

Most traditional churches, or religions, in the developed countries have seen a significant drop in their number of followers. Churches or religions that have enjoyed growth in numbers, and revenue, are those belonging to the evangelical charismatic movement.

A church, with a charismatic leader, and an unlimited amount of passion has the ability to fill a room with positive energy and inspire people to follow his beliefs. The followers are mesmerized and a great leader will develop loyalty and obedience by the strength of his or her personality. It is a form of high emotional energy that excites people to the point of frenzied hyperactive behaviour. People attend these staged events to escape their boring lives, and often leave energized and on an emotional high. It can be addictive.

Many people could care less about the message, but instead they like the performance, the charisma and the atmosphere of induced excitement. It provides an adrenaline rush.

Other churches employ a combination of passionate speeches with high energy music. To attract young people; some churches are experiencing success with Christian rock bands playing at their church services. All of this is an effort to stimulate interest in religion through various means of entertainment. In the meantime, they succeed in drawing people toward a religious dogma that the followers know very little about.

It is not complicated, but it is smart. They know that most people would prefer to watch a movie that is dramatic, and filled with action to get the emotions rising, rather than a dry documentary about the problems of the world. Advertisers and marketing professional have known this for years. If you are going to sell steak, you sell the sizzle not the meat. Your product must be exciting. It must be appealing. Unfortunately, fantasy has much more appeal than facts.

The challenge that the atheist movement; (I don't think it has reached the stage yet when it can be called a movement) faces is - it is not sexy, exciting, or entertaining. If we are to be honest, facts, reality, reason, and evidence is for the most part rather boring. For most people this sounds like too much thinking. For some; thinking hurts. They would rather watch, dance, sing and be entertained, and leave the thinking to others.

Atheism will need to re-examine how to package and present itself to the uninformed public.

Notwithstanding the multitude of recent books, websites and podcasts on the subject, many people simply have not been exposed to atheism. We need more passion, excitement and yes; ways to entertain. We need a modern day Robert G. Ingersoll.

If we are to ensure the world will become a safe, sane and progressive place, we must realize our responsibility, both personal and collectively. If superstition, dogma and religions remain as the dominant force they will surely destroy what hope remains. A world guided by reality, science and humanism is more likely to advance the human race, and sustain our world for future generations than a world guided by superstition, faith and an invisible deity.

If life, in this world, is to thrive and if people expect a future filled with enjoyment, health and happiness, we must accept a new way of thinking. As a world, we must put the prime importance on human values rather than a divine or supernatural being. To believe that God is all-knowing, all-powerful and perfect in everyway is to stifle human progress, and is a cop-out.

We are responsible for our own future, not some mystical being. Humanists; call it atheism if you wish, believe in the potential value and goodness of human beings. Humanists emphasize common human needs, and seek rational ways of solving human problems. We don't pray for help from above. We roll up our sleeves, and get to work solving problems for humanity.

The time has come for many more atheists/humanists to stand up, speak out and stop the insanity. We must find the proper means to get our message out....without the pain, hatred, and torture that religion has inflicted upon this earth. The blood that has been shed, in the name of religion, has soaked too much of our beautiful planet.

Too many throats have been cut, too many children slaughtered. When bullets and bombs replace words and deeds, we are on the path to destruction.

Somehow, someway, truth will prevail. As we search to find the means we must remain free of distortions or false claims that have so infected the message of religion. Perhaps we will see the day when freedom of religion transforms into freedom from religion.

Until that day, when people are free from the chains of superstitious beliefs, may your life be filled with happiness, the joy of wonderment, love, compassion and friendship all of your days. And when your life is over, you will honestly be able to claim that you lived life to the fullest and, in even in a small way, you left your part of the world a little better because of your grace.

~

IMAGINE

Imagine there's no heaven
It's easy if you try
No hell below us
Above us only sky
Imagine all the people
Living for today...

Imagine there's no countries
It isn't hard to do
Nothing to kill or die for
And no religion too
Imagine all the people
Living life in peace...

You may say I'm a dreamer
But I'm not the only one
I hope someday you'll join us
And the world will be as one

Imagine no possessions
I wonder if you can
No need for greed or hunger
A brotherhood of man
Imagine all the people
Sharing all the world...

You may say I'm a dreamer
But I'm not the only one
I hope someday you'll join us
And the world will live as one

-John Lennon

NOTABLE ATHEISTS/HUMANIST WHO HAVE SIGNED THIS BOOK

DAVE FITZGERALD
JOEY KIRKMAN
DAN BARKER
TRACIE HARRIS
ARON RA
JEREMIAH CAMARA
JT EBERHARD
SARAH MOREHEAD
HEMANT MEHTA
RUSSELL GLASSER
CHRISTOPHER DiCARLO
TERESA McBAIN
ERIC THOMAS
DEBORAH McTAGGART
MATT DILLAHUNTY
LUCIEN GREAVES
PZ MYERS
LAURENCE KRAUSE
KARIS BURTOWSKI
VYCKIE GARRISON
REBECCA VITSMUN
DOUG THOMAS
MAAJID NAWAZ